THE POWER OF

PASSIVE INCOME

MAKE YOUR MONEY WORK FOR YOU

Nightingale-Conant

Entrepreneur Press®

Entrepreneur Press, Publisher
Cover Design: Andrew Welyczko
Production and Composition: Eliot House Productions

This publication is designed to provide accurate and authoritative information
in regard to the subject matter covered. It is sold with the understanding that
the publisher is not engaged in rendering legal, accounting, or other professional
services. If legal advice or other expert assistance is required, the services of a
competent professional person should be sought.

Entrepreneur Press® is a registered trademark of Entrepreneur Media, Inc.

Library of Congress Cataloging-in-Publication Data
    Names: Entrepreneur Media, Inc., issuer.
    Title: The power of passive income: make your money work for
       you / by Nightingale-Conant and Entrepreneur Media, Inc.
    Description: Irvine, California: Entrepreneur Media, Inc., [2019]
    Identifiers: LCCN 2018043593 | ISBN 978-1-59918-637-5 (alk. paper) |
       ISBN 1-59918-637-3 (alk. paper)
    Subjects: LCSH: Information technology—Economic aspects. | Electronic
       commerce. | Investments. | Income.
    Classification: LCC HC79.I55 P69 2019 | DDC 332.6—dc23
    LC record available at https://lccn.loc.gov/2018043593

Printed in the United States of America

23 22 21 20 19   10 9 8 7 6 5 4 3 2 1

CONTENTS

FOREWORD

By Robert W. Bly, marketing and passive income expert and author of *The Digital Marketing Handbook, The Marketing Plan Handbook,* and *The Direct Mail Revolution*

The majority of people I meet have basically one stream of income. This is typically a 9-to-5 job where they trade time for money or a small service or retail business they own in which they also trade time for money. Any business, job, or profession where you are paid only when you actually work is "active income." Dentists, for instance, have a saying: "If you're not drilling and filling, you're not billing." As highly paid as they are, dentists only get paid when they are working. If they are not working, they aren't getting paid, which is the drawback of active income.

In this book, you will discover one of the ways to escape the 9-to-5 rat race: Develop one or more streams of "passive income" (money you are making even when you are not working). You could be playing golf, taking your kids to Disneyland, fishing, or just loafing—but with passive income, you are still getting a steady stream of cash with no direct labor on your part.

For instance, if you own an apartment building or multifamily house and hire a property management firm to manage it, you collect rent checks from tenants every month—without lifting a finger. Likewise, if you are an investor and buy 10,000 ounces of silver bullion at $10 an ounce, hold onto it, and then sell when the price hits $30—you have made a $200,000 profit in passive income while sitting on your deck or vacationing in France.

That's why most wealthy people have multiple streams of passive income. That's why you should, too—and *The Power of Passive Income* shows you how to achieve true financial freedom by building one or more passive income streams.

For many years, I have had multiple streams of passive income—including many of those listed in the table of contents of this book. For me personally, my biggest passive income stream is my online business—primarily selling information products on the internet.

A few weeks ago, I checked my email on a Thursday night at around 6 P.M. Nothing important in the inbox. So, our family went to our favorite local Korean restaurant for a quick dinner. When we got home around 8 P.M., I checked my mail inbox again. And here's what I found: While we were out at the restaurant, two of my customers had each ordered multiple information products from me—just in the time it took me to eat dinner.

The total dollar amount: $1,079.65.

Now, that's not a fortune. It didn't make me rich. But the average American between ages 35 and 64 earns around $50,000 a year—or roughly a grand a week. That means that, thanks to just one of my passive income streams, I made in just two hours about the same amount of money the average American earns in a week! A nice little chunk of cash with no labor on my part. No meetings. No phone calls. No going to the office (which is in the house).

I tell you this not to brag, but to make a point: I firmly believe you should have multiple streams of income, with at least one of them—and preferably, most or all of them—being passive income for two reasons.

First, while a paycheck from a 9-to-5 job is steady and expected, orders like the $1,079.65 I made overnight are unexpected—and there is delight in surprise. An unexpected royalty, commission, bonus, profit from the sale of a flip house, a stock that goes up, or a large online order makes my day, and many of my fellow solopreneurs have told me the same is true for them, too.

Second, and more important, if you can develop a passive income stream that generates an annual six-figure income (without regular active daily labor from you), you achieve a degree of financial security that 95 percent of your friends, relatives, and neighbors will never have.

I am not money hungry or even money oriented. I work long hours in my freelance copywriting business, which is my primary active income stream, and will do so as long as I am able because I love it.

But by making a six-figure passive second income online, it's comforting to know I could live nicely off that income stream alone if I so desired. And by following the advice in this book, *The Power of Passive Income*, you will discover how to set yourself free from the need to work for someone else—making them rich in the process—and make *yourself* rich instead.

INTRODUCTION

Welcome to Entrepreneur Media presents *The Power of Passive Income*. For the first time, we are partnering with Nightingale-Conant, the world's largest producer of audio programs and the world leader in personal development content, to bring you an exclusive look at the proven techniques you need to create a passive income stream. This hands-on guide from Nightingale-Conant is designed to maximize your income, minimize your stress level, and get the absolute most from every moment of your life while also sharing the tips, tricks, and techniques you've come to trust from the

Entrepreneur brand. It's a winning combination that we hope will help you win, too.

These are ambitious goals, so as a way of getting started, let's look for a moment at what getting the most from your life really means. The fact is, over the course of a year, most Americans spend more time working than they do in any other activity. You may spend a day at the beach with your family, or you may even go on a two-week vacation, but in the overall context of your life, those are just interludes. On the whole, day in and day out, month after month, most people are hard at work. What's more, the percentage of our time that we spend working has dramatically increased over the past two decades. Compared to the way we used to work and also compared to other nations of the world, Americans are workaholics. We may not like it or we may have never even stopped to think about it, but that's the way things are in the 21st century.

Of course, if we're going to talk about work, we need to know exactly what "work" means—and for most people the definition is quite clear. It doesn't matter whether you're a brain surgeon or a carpenter, a taxi driver or a trial lawyer; the fact is, work is really a matter of trading time for money. True, sometimes the trade is better than others. Some people get a lot of money for their time, while others get less. But those differences are superficial compared to the basic unifying fact: Most of us are selling our time and the effort or skill with which we fill that time. It's that simple.

But there's a problem. None of us has an unlimited amount of time to sell. In fact, everybody has exactly the same amount of time. The only difference is how much we can sell it for. Over the course of a lifetime—by getting a good education, by developing a unique skill, and especially by working hard—we can increase our income. But sooner or later, we reach the limit. Sooner or later, we're as good as we can be at our chosen profession. Sooner or later, we're charging as much money as the market can bear. And sooner or later, we just can't work any harder.

If you've reached that point or even if you can just begin to see it looming on the horizon, this book is for you. You'll learn about some of the proven, practical ways of earning income beyond the limits of the clock and the calendar. Instead of selling your time and talents to whatever buyers you can find, you'll have buyers looking for you at every moment of the day. That's the real meaning of the term *passive income*, which you'll be reading about throughout this book. But it's not really the income that's passive at all. The income is very active— as active as you can make it. *You* are really the passive element in passive income, because all you have to do is collect. In fact, once you really get your passive income streams in place, collecting income can literally be *all* you have to do. True, it will take some time and effort to get there, but you really can achieve total self-sufficiency from passive income. Lots of people are doing it, and you can, too.

HOW TO USE THIS BOOK

First, let's talk about what this book is *not*. This is not an all-encompassing, step-by-step, everything-you-need-to-know guide to every type of passive income opportunity listed in this book. Quite frankly, every single one of the options you'll read about is deserving of its own how-to book. There simply isn't enough room here to cover every single step you need to take to successfully run one of these passive income gigs.

Rather, the goal of this book is to walk you through the main tenets of the passive income lifestyle, help you assess your personal goals, and introduce you to some of the best paths toward passive income success. You will read about what it takes to get into the passive income mindset and how to clearly define what *you* want to achieve so you can choose a passive income model that works for your lifestyle. Then, we'll walk you through various options for earning passive income and creating a long-term plan that will get you out of an office cubicle for good and onto a golf course, in a plane, or on a beach. Finally, we'll talk about some long-term strategies for no-fuss wealth building that will ensure you get to stay on that beach for the long run.

Now settle in, grab a cup of coffee and something to take notes with, and get ready to discover the power of passive income!

CHAPTER ONE

LAYING THE GROUNDWORK

Before you get to know all of the many ways you can make passive income work for you, we are going to talk about some of the basics behind the power of passive income. Let's start with the name of it—passive income. The word "passive" sometimes gets a bad rap. We are urged to be active participants in our lives, not passively let life happen to us. That's a fair point, and it's a useful rule to follow. After all, you are the driver of your destiny, and only you can make success happen. However, when it comes to making money, there is a power in doing so passively. In other words, getting the most bang for your buck with the least effort. Wouldn't it be great to have an income stream (or two, or three) that, once set up, brought in money for you while you were doing other things? Of course! Think of the time you could spend doing what you like with the people you love if you had an income stream that was doing most of the work for you. That's the power of passive income!

The amazing thing is, huge numbers of people don't know that passive income even exists. If you're one of those people, you work hard for your money, and in order to have more money, you think you may have to work even harder. Since there's a good chance that's how you see things right now, try making a radical change in your perceptions—let's call it a paradigm shift. It's more than just changing the way you earn money or gain income. It's a transformation in the way you see money itself. It's seeing wealth and success in entirely new ways.

Right now, for example, perhaps you see wealth in terms of a dollar amount. Let's consider a quick scenario. Say Mr. Smith has $20 million, so he's wealthy. Mr. Jones is $20,000 in debt, so he's the opposite of wealthy. But a number is just a number—it's not true wealth (or lack thereof). For our purposes here, we're going to ask you to take the price tag off wealth. Instead of thinking in terms of thousands or millions or billions, we're going to be talking about freedom and fulfillment and creativity. That doesn't mean you're not going to be making more money—because you definitely are. However, you're going to make that because you've learned how to see money very differently than before.

KNOW YOUR "WHY"

In this book, we're going to be asking and answering a lot more "what" questions than "why" questions. For example, we're going to talk about *what* you can do to start an online business or *what* you'll need to develop income from real estate. But here at the start there are a few *why* questions that need to be answered. Once you've got those answers in place, the tools and tactics of passive income will be a lot more effective.

So, ask yourself why you want more income. For a lot of people, that may seem like a foolish question. Wanting more money is just hardwired into us, isn't it? It's like the old saying: You can't be too thin or too rich. But if you think about it, money is never really an end in itself. The desire for wealth is something different from just wanting to hold a lot of bills in your hand. For some people, money means access to material possessions, whether it's a big yacht or fine watch or just a nice house to live in. For others, wealth means security. It's not having to worry about how you're going to pay the mortgage or fund your children's education. All those things are very worthwhile expressions of wealth.

THE NEW MEANING OF WEALTH

For our purposes, however, we're going to suggest a slightly different way of thinking of wealth. At least initially, your goal in creating passive income will not be the same as the other financial objectives you set for yourself. In one word, what we're going to achieve here is *freedom*—freedom from the need to keep earning more, working harder, and trying to sell your time to the highest bidder. The passive income streams you create are going to relieve that pressure. Once the pressure is relieved, you'll have much greater freedom to make key decisions in your life—both financially and in every other area.

Right now, you may be in the position of having to take every assignment that comes along. For good reason, you may be unwilling to think about making a job change or a career transformation— because you're worried about missing a paycheck. In your heart, you may still have larger financial hopes and dreams, but right now you're in bondage. You're tied to the time-for-money framework, and within that framework, your options are very limited. Creating passive income will take you outside that box. Bondage will be replaced by freedom. Instead of just meeting your financial needs, you'll begin to make your own financial choices.

This is an extremely important point, so let's make sure we're clear about it. It's great to have lofty, long-term financial goals—but it's going to be hard to achieve them if your single income stream goes to just maintaining the lifestyle you have now. Passive income streams will give you the liberty to pursue your goals more aggressively. It's certainly true that the passive income ideas we'll be talking about can themselves become major income sources—but initially they are sources of freedom. They'll give you the freedom to look at the big picture of your financial life, to see the opportunities, and to act on them immediately.

FIND YOUR FREEDOM

By now you're probably starting to see that the concept of passive income is a major viewpoint shift. Within the time-for-money equation, most people spend their whole lives trying to achieve a big income. They think a big income will make them rich. But a big income is worth little if expenses are just as big. People who are still working harder and harder to sell time for money are not really living the life of wealthy individuals, no matter how big the numbers are.

This leads to a second shift in viewpoint. We've said that our initial goal for passive income is financial freedom. If you're like most people, this is a goal that will be attained incrementally over time. You may not be able to quit your day job immediately—you may not even want to quit it—but as your passive income increases, your dependence on your day job will decrease. Ultimately, of course, passive income can liberate you from needing to work at all. You may still choose to work, but that's very different from needing to.

But here's the point: Whether this happens will depend not only on the amount of your passive income, but on how you spend it. To help understand this, there's a well-established principle of workplace behavior called Parkinson's Law. This principle states that the time needed to complete a particular task will expand to fill the time available. If people have a two-week deadline to complete a report, the vast majority of them will take two weeks to do it—not because they need that much time, but because that's how much time they have. If they had a week to do the report or if they had a month, they would get it done in that time, too.

For the vast majority of people, spending works the same way, or almost the same way. If we have a $100, we find ways to spend a $100— or maybe $110. We live in a mindset of instant gratification, so as soon as we have the means to gratify ourselves, we do it. But if you can get out of that mindset, it's actually possible to start building wealth even with a significantly lower income.

GET OUT OF THE DEBT HOLE

Before we go any further, it's important to address an issue that affects millions of Americans. Here's how one entrepreneur described this issue: "When I learned about passive income, I was immediately eager to get started. But there was a problem. I didn't have any working capital—and I mean not *any*. In fact, I had over $20,000 in credit card debt. I knew that, obviously, that was going to make things very difficult. So, the first order of business was to get out of that hole."

That hole of consumer debt—credit card debt in particular—can paralyze you financially even if you're totally up to speed in every other way. You can be motivated, intelligent, creative, and everything else, but if you're having to service debt every month, you're not going to have the small initial investment capital you need. You don't need a lot of assets to create passive income, but you do need some. You can't afford to be paying credit card bills with money that could be going toward your financial freedom. Passive expenses are just as real as passive income—and credit card debt is the ultimate passive expense. So let's take a quick look at how to get rid of it.

The first step is a bit of honest self-assessment. Many people feel so badly about their consumer debt that they actually don't know how much they have. They'd rather not think about it, so they just pay the bills every month and put it out of their thoughts. That's not the way to make credit card debt go away, however. Start by determining exactly how much you owe. Frightening as that may seem, you'll actually feel better once you have a dollars-and-cents figure to deal with. If it's any consolation, you can be sure there are millions of people who are in exactly the same boat. Well, you're going to get out of that boat starting today.

One of the challenges of consumer debt is that it can get started quickly, but getting out of debt can take time. You can put a thousand dollars on your credit card in just a few seconds—then you can be stuck with that debt for months or years. The truth is, beating debt is a gradual process, and it can seem especially slow at the beginning. But have faith. Signs of progress will begin to appear, and gradually they will begin to multiply. And remember: As you get rid of your passive expenses, your options for passive income will start to open up. Even if you don't realize it at first, you'll already be closer to the freedom that passive income represents.

When you're first beginning to attack your debt, it's important to eliminate as many unnecessary expenses as possible. In other words, the best way to build passive income when in debt is to get rid of passive expenses. This means eliminating whatever is taking your money each month while you sleep, including interest payments on credit cards, car loans, and any other recurring bills you might have. For the moment, you will want to organize your lifestyle so that your monthly expenses are at the absolute minimum. Think of this as a tactical maneuver, not a permanent condition. Because if you follow this plan, the day will soon come when you'll get everything back and more—plus, you'll really be able to afford it.

We're not going to spend a lot of time on debt issues, because the facts are pretty straightforward. There aren't really any secrets, and the solution is just common sense. Cut back or eliminate your credit card purchases, transfer high-interest debt to lower interest accounts, and try to pay at least twice the minimum balances each month—starting with the highest-interest debts. Think of this process as a test of your commitment to success. As your debt shrinks, your working capital will grow. Before you know it—in months, not years—you'll have the nest egg you need to really build passive income.

INVEST IN YOUR NEST (EGG)

If you'd like to have an exact figure of what it will take to get started on building your passive income stream, $5,000 is more than enough. Keep in mind that you can get started with a bit more or a bit less. But $5,000 is a doable initial investment for most (once any debt is out of the way), so let's run with it. Once you have that amount of money to invest in your initial moves to build passive income, you're really ready to go. Assuming you're at that point now, keep in mind the principles we've discussed. First, wealth is not based on a dollar amount. Second, we tend to spend everything we have, whether it's on consumer purchases or consumer debt. These principles affect not only our day-to-day experiences in the retail marketplace, but also our investment behavior. For example, when people start saving for retirement, it's not unusual for them to set a goal of $1 million. They keep putting money into a 401(k) or some other investment vehicle until they reach the $1 million target. Then, several different things can happen. A certain number of people will think they have so much money that they start spending the principal. They may not spend very much at first, but it adds up. There's a kind of self-sabotaging mechanism in this. Something similar often afflicts lottery winners, because studies have shown that many winners end up spending their jackpot in two years or less.

But suppose an individual doesn't spend the million dollars that's accrued over the years. Even if they keep it in dividend-producing stocks or treasury bonds, the payout is relatively low. If you choose a conservative strategy, which is what most advisors would recommend, you could expect to earn about 5 percent annually. That's approximately $4,000 per month. It's not an inconsiderable sum. It can definitely help achieve the kind of financial freedom we're talking about. But if all you've done during your career is fund your IRA that freedom has probably come at the price of many decades of bondage. In this book, we're going to show you how to do considerably better than that, and without increasing your risk.

MANAGE YOUR INCOME—AND EXPECTATIONS

A key piece of information in passive income is the amount of money you need to live without working. Clearly, there are two factors to consider here: how can you maximize your income, and how can you manage your spending? If you have very extravagant tastes, the amount of money you need will obviously have to be larger. You just need to be aware of that fact. It doesn't mean you have to live in a cardboard box now to benefit from passive income later, but you shouldn't expect to be buying private jets, either. Anyone who tells you differently is not being honest with you—and one thing we're going to be in this book is honest.

Simply put, the ultimate goal is for your passive income streams to be greater than your expenses. When that happens, you're free to do anything you want with your time, and your bills will still be paid. Needless to say, you're also free to keep working in order to become really wealthy if you so choose. But you don't *have* to do anything. That's the objective—and you will achieve it as long as you know how to leverage the income (and other assets, like time) that you already have.

LEARN ABOUT YOUR LEVERAGE

In creating passive income, there's one word you should always keep in mind—*leverage*. In financial terms, leverage is the ability to multiply an asset without increasing your investment or your risk. This is especially important for people who are building passive income without much capital at the outset.

There are lots of ways to do this. Let's consider real estate as an example. which we'll be discussing in more detail later in the book. Bestselling authors like Robert Kiyosaki and Bob Allen have done great work in showing how passive income can be developed in that area. As they've pointed out, it's possible to buy a $100,000 house with a down payment of only $5,000. That means you can leverage $5,000 into control of a $100,000 asset. If the house appreciates 5 percent per year, you'll recover your investment after only 12 months, and then you'll continue to get $5,000 for every year that follows. But that's not all. There are a number of other variables that can work for you in real estate. Suppose you're able to buy a single-family rental property for no money down, and you find a tenant who pays enough rent to cover the monthly expenses. You may not make much profit in terms of cash flow, but there's also a good chance that the house will increase in value—and by the end of a year, you'll have paid down part of the mortgage. Through the power of leverage, you've gained significant assets with no investment except your signature.

Time can also be leveraged, just like money—and since freeing your time is one of our major goals, knowing how to do this is a key skill. There are several ways that time can be leveraged. For example, you can hire an employee or maybe even more than one.

Now it may seem like you'll need to have a real up-and-coming business before you can begin taking on staff, but this isn't always true. One very successful entrepreneur—let's call him Richard—had almost nothing in the way of inventory when he began hiring employees and building an income stream. He had no office and no business cards. All he had was a copy of a very old and very charming cookbook that he found at a flea market. Richard took it to a full-service copying center and had some bound copies made. He even added a nicely designed but inexpensive cover. Then Richard ran a very small ad in the newspaper of a local university. The ad said that he was looking for students to work part time doing canvassing work. It also said that there was the potential for very good pay, and that the students could make their own hours. So far his total expenses were about $150.

Although it was pretty obvious from the ad that there would be some selling involved, Richard had plenty of responses. The selling was so low-key that it really could be called canvassing, and the flexible hours also were attractive to college students. When he met with the applicants, Richard told them that their task would be very simple. Each student would be given a cookbook. They were then instructed to approach as many prospects as they could with the following offer. Each prospect was to be given a copy of the book to keep and use for a week. At the end of the week, the prospect could buy the cookbook outright for $15—but if he or she happened to find two other people who wanted cookbooks for $15, the original prospect could keep the book for free. There really was no selling involved on the part of the college students. They just had to describe the offer to as many people as they could—and then, at the end of the two-week period, they could keep 20 percent of whatever money came in.

The success of this plan was amazing. Richard was soon moving hundreds of books, and the only work for him was calling the print center to order more books. But he never got them printed until the orders had actually been placed, so there was still no inventory. And the college students, motivated by the high commission fee, were very creative and aggressive. They targeted front-office employees in office buildings, people working in cafes, and some even went door-to-door to meet retired people and stay-at-home parents. Soon, Richard was able to take more employees into outlying areas of the city. He had virtually no out-of-pocket costs, and soon his time was 100 percent leveraged. He didn't even need to do the initial meeting with new employees. He gave that responsibility to one of his original student workers.

Richard created a passive income stream by leveraging his time in ways that were very powerful but were also decidedly "low tech." He hired living, breathing human beings for tasks that required actual leg work. With the possible exception of the copying technology, there is no reason why Richard's business could not have done just as well 20 years ago or even 50 years ago.

There are many other low-tech options for leveraging your time and money, but the high-tech options may be even more exciting. For example, when you understand the strategies and tactics of passive income through the internet, you can have dozens of income streams with almost no expense, no employees, and very little time at the keyboard. This will be our focus in Chapter 3. We'll see how some of the greatest fortunes started out as passive income vehicles on the internet and explore why your success is built on more than imitating those who came before you. It's built on your enthusiasm for what you love. You'll explore what really interests you—what you really love—and then you'll see how it can make money for you online, even while you're sleeping. But first you need to figure out how to break the cycle of what's been holding you back from creating your own passive income plan.

CHAPTER TWO

BREAKING YOUR BARRIERS

There are lots of ways to build passive income, but all of them depend on a conceptual shift you'll need to make as soon as possible. You'll need to start thinking in a fundamentally new way about money and how to get it.

Right now, let's take a look at exactly what this means by exploring five basic differences between passive income and the traditional time-for-money model. As you read about each one, ask yourself where you stand with respect to each point. There are several different possibilities. For example, you may already feel completely comfortable with the passive income philosophy. Or you may need to get beyond your present mindset, which may require some creative thinking on your part. As you read in the opening chapter, accurate self-assessment is very important. Then, after we've looked at the five points in this chapter, we'll see how they connect to our topic in the next chapter, which is creating passive income online.

PASSIVE INCOME VS. TIME-FOR-MONEY MODEL

"But it's all income!" they say. "Income is income—it all spends the same!" Well, yes and no. First off, if "they" don't support you and your desire to make a better, richer life for yourself, then get them out of your head. This is your journey, not theirs. And because this is your journey, what *you* want needs to be front and center of your plan to make passive income work for you. With that in mind, let's look at the five differences between the two models and how they relate to your goals:

1. Passive income works best when you focus on what you know and what you love. The traditional model, on the other hand, focuses on what the marketplace wants to buy.

2. Passive income means that the amount of money you make is not tied to the amount of time you work. In the time-for-money model, if you work six hours, you get paid for six hours. With passive income, your earnings are not directly tied to a time commitment.

3. Under the traditional model, you should try to work as hard as you can—because in theory, the harder you work, the more money you'll make. But one of the most important objectives of passive income is to work as little as possible. Since there is no direct connection between your amount of passive income and the time you work, freedom from work itself is a logical goal.

4. Time for money means there is a limit to the amount of income you can generate. Depending on your line of work, this may be higher or lower, but there's *always* a limit. A corporate lawyer might make $300 an hour, but there are still only so many hours

in a day. But there is literally no limit to the money that can come from a successful passive income business.

5. In the traditional time-for-money paradigm, the goal is retirement after an extended working career. It may be 20 years, 30 years, or even longer than that, but the plan is to build up enough capital so you can stop working. The returns from that capital may come to you in the form of a pension or as payments from a retirement fund. But the money that you've accumulated is going to be supporting you. With passive income, however, the goal is to stop working as soon as possible, if you so choose. You may want to keep having a full- or part-time job, but you won't need one in order to meet your expenses. You'll be supported by the revenue streams you've created—not by the fixed income of pensions or retirement funds. In fact, your passive income streams should be the opposite of fixed. Those streams should be growing continually. They should provide not only financial freedom, but also more options and opportunities in every area of your life.

One of the most interesting things about financial success is the way people have mixed feelings about it—feelings that they might not even know they have. Sure, we all say we'd like to be wealthy, but underneath the desire for wealth there's often a certain degree of subconscious conflict. Do we think rich people are good people? Very often, we don't—and whether we realize it or not, most of us would rather be good than rich. And if there's a sense that a person has become rich without having earned that wealth through honest labor, the negative ideas we attach to that wealth become even stronger. Yet here we are talking about how passive income can bring revenue without you doing any work, and what a good thing that is.

YOUR FINANCIAL BELIEF SYSTEM

Have you ever really explored your beliefs about money and how to get it? If you're like the vast majority of people, those beliefs didn't come to you by choice. Instead, over the course of many years, you absorbed the pre-existing beliefs of our society. One of these, as we've mentioned, is the idea that "work is its own reward." Another is the general scarcity consciousness of "there's not enough" and or the fear consciousness of "disaster could happen at any moment." The bottom line is, you may have grown up with the idea that "money is dangerous" or even "money is evil." If that's the case, then chances are you're not going to bring a great deal of money into your life. But no matter what your beliefs are or where they come from, you have the power to create new beliefs to accomplish your financial goals.

Please don't misunderstand. You don't need to work through a moral crisis to feel OK about some extra income. But you should understand how radically different this is from concepts of wealth that are deeply ingrained in our society. Consider the idea that "work is its own reward," for example. Basically, this means that people benefit from hard work whether or not they make any money from it. This may be very true in terms of an individual's spiritual development— but work is definitely not its own reward when it comes to someone's financial standing. With respect to passive income, we can make an even more extreme statement. In mathematical terms, this extreme statement can be made in just a few words: Work and passive income vary indirectly. In other words, if you spend a lot of time working, your passive income is likely to be low. But if you spend very little time working, your passive income is probably high and getting higher. So, for our purposes here, you'll want to embrace the idea that hard work is not necessarily the way to success.

AVOID SELF-SABOTAGE

Right now, let's look at some of the self-sabotaging beliefs people hold about money—and let's also see how to replace those beliefs with new ideas for building real wealth.

One of the most widespread beliefs is that making money is very difficult. It's too hard and complicated for the average person. You've got to be a genius like Bill Gates, right? But the truth is, millions of people have become wealthy and millions more are going to do it in the very near future. You can be one of them. If you *want* to do it, you *can* do it.

There are also many people who tell themselves that they don't like to think about money. They might enjoy having more of it, but they don't really want to focus on it. They tell themselves that maybe, if they don't really concentrate on it, wealth will come into their lives all by itself. But in reality, we all have to think about money whether we want to or not. And the less we have of it, the more we have to think about it. We all have to pay the electric bill, pay the mortgage, put our kids through school, and a thousand other things. So, remember: The passive income streams you can build aren't ends in themselves. They're vehicles for setting you free in a financial sense. Once you're free, you can stop thinking about money altogether if you so desire. Or you can think about it more than ever and in completely new ways. But the choices won't be forced upon you. You will make your own decisions about the place of money in your life.

Another common belief is the idea that making money involves luck or that it requires special abilities. This is the idea that wealth happens by chance. It's a matter of being in the right place at the right time. You just have to be lucky; and if you're not lucky, there's nothing you can do about it. But would you say that the top individuals in any field got there just because they're lucky? Does a baseball player hit a home run just because they were lucky enough to get a good pitch? Does a poker player win a world championship just because they got the right cards? It's true that chance plays a part, but you've got to be able to make the most of the chances that come your way.

It can definitely be useful to think of making money as a game, but there's more to it than just rolling the dice. The game of making money is challenging and fun, and it becomes more fun once you learn how to play it well. And the amazing thing is, you can even teach the money-making game to play itself. That's really what passive income is all about.

It's not wrong or unspiritual to want to earn money without working hard for every single penny. Your prosperity does not detract from anyone else's. The world is a place of abundant opportunity, and we should be grateful for the chance to put those to work. Wanting to be financially successful is not wrong. It's perfectly natural. And since you are a good person, you will put your money to good use. So, the more money you have, the better the world will be.

Now that we've gotten past the unconscious barriers that people place between themselves and financial success, we're ready to start looking at how to build passive income in the most exciting medium ever created in the history of humankind. Yes, that's a big statement, but that's exactly what the internet is.

CHAPTER THREE

RAMPING UP FOR ONLINE SUCCESS

Getting started on a passive income strategy is as easy as logging on to your computer. From setting up a simple blog site that includes advertising or affiliate marketing or diving deep into the creation of an ecommerce site where you will sell digital or physical products, there are endless opportunities for earning passive income online.

If your only experience with online businesses is by way of looking at landing pages for general company information or online shopping, then you have some catching up to do. There can often be a learning curve involved for anyone who is used to traditional business models. But part of that learning curve includes a very important fact. Yes, internet-based business can be very different in many ways from a traditional brick-and-mortar (or, as we call it, the time-for-money model), but in some ways it's not nearly as different as you might think. Knowing what's unique about online commerce is only useful if you also know what's *not* unique.

So, how do you hatch your online idea? There are two basic ways that successful businesses get started in any field, and internet businesses are no different. The first way involves a couple of people sitting down at the proverbial kitchen table and trying to think of a great way to get rich. For some reason, this is rarely done by a single individual. It's usually people who have known each other for a while and who know each other's strengths and weaknesses. Google, for example, was started by two friends—Sergei Brin and Larry Page—who understood the moneymaking potential of a dominant search engine. Internet search engines weren't their favorite hobby. Instead, search engines were the vehicle they wanted to use for building wealth. And it really worked!

But it usually doesn't work. For every Google jackpot, there are millions of brainstorming jackasses who got nowhere. That's why it's usually a red flag when someone says, "I've got a great idea that's going to make a lot of money." If the only reason it's a great idea is because you think it's going to make a lot of money, you're probably wrong on both counts. It's probably not going to make a lot of money, so it probably isn't a great idea, either.

HARNESS THE POWER OF YOUR INTERESTS

Now consider the second way businesses get started (which is a much more encouraging picture, by the way). Unlike the two-person, get-rich scenario, this one usually involves just one person—you. It begins with asking yourself a few simple questions:

→ What am I really interested in?
→ What do I know about?

◦— What do I care about?

◦— What do I *love*?

At the outset, the answers you come up with are less important than the positive energy you attach to them. If you're really interested in the career statistics of 19th century baseball players, that's great. Make a note of it. You may think that nobody else could possibly care about who played first base for Mudville in 1886, but you'd be surprised. There are probably at least 10,000 people who are as interested in old-time baseball as you are. But what's different now is that you can find out who those people are. You can connect with them almost immediately. And there's a good chance that you can translate that connection into a passive income stream. It might make you rich someday, or it might not. But what it can certainly do is assist you in meeting your financial responsibilities, which means greater freedom for you to concentrate on other things. Remember, freedom is our first goal in creating passive income.

Here's how to go about it—and this is where the internet comes in. Once you've identified your unique interests, you can start searching for every possible link to that interest on the internet. You can see if there are any clubs of baseball fanatics who like to play games in 19th century uniforms. You can search for people who have an interest in baseball statistics, which is actually a huge demographic. You can see which websites touch on your interest, even if it's only in a very minor way—and then you can get ready to access the members' database.

For the moment, think about the uniqueness of your interest, not the scale of it. Want an example? A hundred years ago, Henry Ford wanted every family in America to own a Model T. In the 1980s, Bill Gates said that Microsoft's goal was to get a personal computer into every home in America. Those are big ideas. Big ideas are great, and they can be very profitable. But they're also harder to come up with, and they're more complicated because your potential customers are more diverse. You may have to work harder to find the common interest. In fact, you may even have to create an interest where one doesn't exist initially.

In any case, the fact that your idea may begin on a small scale doesn't mean it can't make money. And your idea may actually be much bigger than you think. So once you've identified your interest and done some research on it, you're ready to start building on that. You're ready to make the connection between what interests *you* and what *other people* find interesting. There are times when it's easy to make that jump, and other times when it's more difficult. But one thing is certain: The more sharply focused your idea is, the easier it is to translate into some level of passive income.

CHOOSING AN ONLINE MODEL THAT IS RIGHT FOR YOU

When you're first getting started, try to choose the online income model with the lowest barrier to entry. This is especially true if you have a strong need for a short-term cash infusion so you can ramp up your online income stream for long-term success. For this reason, most of the time when starting out, the answer to the question about how you will create an online business will largely go hand-in-hand with whether you start off selling services or products.

The determining factors are different for everyone. Do you have a skill that you can easily freelance with if you just knew how? Are you connected to a specific market that would jump-start your efforts to sell a product in that industry? Have you already developed a product but have no idea how to market it? Your situation is unique to you, so it makes sense that the smartest path to start on will be unique to you as well.

It might sound silly, but many people don't know which online models naturally have the lowest barrier to entry. It's not something they have had cause to think about. People tend to put all the focus of their research and analysis on one idea, with little to no assessment of themselves and whether the opportunity they are looking at is an ideal fit for them. Let's consider two questions that are designed to evaluate which opportunities are the most suitable for you so you can make the best possible decisions.

Remember, there are no wrong answers, and whatever you select right now doesn't need to be permanent or exclusive. Our advice is to answer based on your gut instinct. The important thing is to be honest, so you can select an online income stream you will have the most success with.

These two questions are designed to help you identify which option appeals to you the most:

- Do you like the idea of being your own boss and working for yourself by leveraging talents and skills that you already have to make money online?
- Do you like the idea of owning your own business by setting up an online revenue stream that you will operate and manage but doesn't necessarily monetize your personal skill set?

What did you find out? Did your answers surprise you? Are you now thinking of yourself as a passive business owner, as opposed to an employee or hands-on startup entrepreneur? If so, you're one step ahead of the game because you're able to make the distinction and realize which one is most attractive to you.

ASSESSING YOUR PERSONAL SKILLS, RESOURCES, AND LIFESTYLE

Some people are great at assessing themselves. Some people are great at evaluating opportunities. However, most need some guidance to discover which opportunities are the best match for them and their goals when it comes to choosing an online business model.

If you want to be the best *you* in this new online passive income adventure, you're going to need to be on the level about what your strengths and weaknesses are. Go in with your eyes open, knowing what you're good at, where you're lacking, and what your non-negotiables are.

Personal Skills and Talents

Everyone has marketable skills. That doesn't mean your marketable skills will have anything to do with what kind of online business model you choose. By creating a portfolio of your skills and talents that you share online or with potential business partners or investors (or even a short list) as you evaluate different opportunities, you'll be able to more quickly assess what you will need to hire or acquire to be successful, and whether it is realistic for you at this time.

Everything should be taken into consideration. This should be a fact-based list without emotion attached to it. Even if you don't understand how a particular skill or experience could be beneficial, write it down.

Your Relationship with Your Skills

Now that you have an impartial list of your skills and talents, you get to rate them based on how much you enjoy doing each of them. Next to each talent or skill, rate it on a scale of 1 to 5.

1. I *love* doing this.
2. It's not my first choice, but I'm good at it, so if it needs to get done, I can do it.
3. I'm neutral. I could take it or leave it.
4. While I'm good at this, I don't want to do it for long.
5. I'd rather do anything other than do this skill for any length of time.

One of the reasons this is so important is that being in business for yourself has a lot of unexpected twists and turns. No matter how well you plan, once you put yourself in a role or place a responsibility on your plate, you may get stuck there for much longer than you anticipate. In addition, most entrepreneurial-minded people have difficulty, at least in the beginning, of letting go of responsibilities they do well. But part of passive income success is doing just that. It's a hindrance to believe that no one will ever do it as well as you, so therefore you will never be able to pass it off. Be realistic about how you feel about your strengths, so that if you end up supplying that skill for longer than you planned, your business or lifestyle doesn't suffer. People who enjoy what they do get things done faster and more efficiently and are happier in general.

Being aware of the skills you bring to the table and how you feel about each of them helps you make long- and short-term decisions and set goals. It gives you clarity about whom you might need to hire and helps you evaluate which areas of your passive business you may need to build with financing vs. using your own sweat equity. It helps you make outsourcing and partnering decisions that will greatly impact how you view your implementation timelines and processes, depending on how much work you want to do yourself using your own skill set and how much you want to outsource.

Hobbies, Passions, and Experience

One thing that is really exciting about being an online entrepreneur is that often the paths with the lowest barriers to entry center on topics you are already familiar with. Making money online is exciting. Making money online about a topic you love is even better. That's when your work doesn't feel like work. For this reason, listing the hobbies, interests, and topics you're experienced in is really helpful. When you're evaluating some of these ideas, already being aware of niches and industries that you have some advanced knowledge of will be helpful to you.

There is no interest that doesn't count. Most (if not all) things have monetizable areas. While you are getting ready to make your own list, here are a few ideas to help you brainstorm:

- *Hobbies.* Do you have hobbies about which you are passionate? Perhaps you belly dance or sail, or are really into massively multi-player online role-playing games like Fortnite. Do you show dogs? Do you run a playgroup for moms? Are you an artist? Do you play any sports? Do you love to travel? Are you an avid photographer? Do you sew? Any area of interest is fair game online.
- *Education.* Do you have a degree or certification in anything? Do you have a psychology degree? Are you a certified doula? Did you get a certification or training program in something else?
- *Profession.* Are you or were you at any time a nurse? Have you worked as a dental hygienist? Did you work in a flower shop and can make wicked flower arrangements? Do you have experience

in event planning? Have you worked in real estate off and on your whole life?

- *Everyday life.* Are you a fashionista? Do you follow the current music scene? Are you interested in politics? Are you a parent? Are you a corporate executive? Are you an extreme couponer?

These are just a few examples to get your juices flowing. If you have something you are passionate about or interested in, there are tons of other people who are, too.

Financial Resources

There's a good chance you might respond to any suggestion to evaluate how many financial resources you have to devote to your new endeavor with a resounding "If I had extra money lying around, I wouldn't be reading this book." So, before we talk about how much money you do or don't have available, let's make a deal about how we will think about money during this exercise.

Not having as much money as you want is never pleasant. Whether your annual income is $30,000 or $30 million, it's simply distressing. But as you read in Chapter 2 try to have a positive relationship with money. As long as you are focusing on how much you don't have and how much pressure and stress that places on you, then you can't be fully present to evaluate how you can improve your situation.

You're probably familiar with the phrase "It takes money to make money." There is definitely truth to that, but that does *not* mean you have to pull money out of your pockets before you make your first dollar. So, there is a message of encouragement here. Yes, it almost always takes money to make money, but there are a lot of ways to start on your path with very little initial investment. That said, as you're building your online passive income plan, you should take inventory on what capital you could draw from should you need or choose to.

Having a clear understanding of what resources you have to draw from enables you to evaluate opportunities properly so you don't get in over your head and end up in a worse situation than you started in.

It also gives you the foundation of a plan to create the money you need when a worthy cause presents itself. Finally, when you have limited resources, you want to make sure you are applying them where they will have the greatest impact on moving you toward your goals of sustainable profitability.

Time

Time is by far one of the most precious, sought-after commodities you possess. It takes time to build an online business. You may not think of your time as a currency, but you absolutely must while working to make passive money online. To most people, their time is more valuable than money. It must be treated as the treasure it really is.

How much time do you realistically have to spend each week creating your passive online business? Can you carve out one hour per week? Two? Five? More?

It's not enough to know how much time you could devote to this; it's equally (if not more) important to have a plan for where you're going to get that time.

If the opportunity were good enough, could you temporarily devote more time to creating your online business? Remember, no is an acceptable answer. The point of this process is to know what resources you have available and how you would get them if you needed or chose to.

People make the mistake of thinking that money is worth more to them than time when starting a business with few resources. But it's more likely that time is an easier sacrifice to make because you literally don't have access to more cash. It's not that people value their time less; it's that their goal is important enough to sacrifice their precious time for the short term so they have more freedom in the long term.

Balance

You do not have infinite balance. No one does! Busy, driven people get worn down. The more you are balancing on your plate, the more patience (also a commodity you need) will be demanded of you. You can add to this list positivity, coping skills, and energy—these are critical in all areas of your lives.

How will you stay balanced, and how will you know when you're not? It can be helpful to write down what is important to you when it comes to maintaining balance and what might be red flags that your life has shifted off balance in a way that isn't acceptable. Sometimes you will choose to run with your time and resources unbalanced in the short term to get a dream off the ground. That's OK. The point is that you're doing it deliberately.

Support

Who is your support system? Is it a spouse? A best friend? Does your dog help you stay balanced and happy? Who can you lean on? Who is a resounding voice of reason that can help you evaluate what you're doing and how you're doing it when things get stressful? Everyone needs a support structure, even when you are focused on making passive, not active, income). So who is on your team?

What Are Your Deal Breakers?

Finally, think about your deal breakers and/or limitations. We all have them. You may not want to spend time on your online business during the weekends because they are reserved for family time. Or perhaps you know that you only want to run an online business dedicated to selling fair trade goods. We all have our requirements and limits that are non-negotiable. Know your limits and don't compromise.

We might have already covered some of your deal breakers. For example, you may have an allotted amount of time you are willing to devote to your online business, and if it consistently requires more time than that, then it's not a good match for you. After all, the goal is for this to be passive income, eventually.

So, what are your non-negotiable and personal limitations? This is especially important. It's very disheartening to get halfway into a new passive income business and realize it's not going to work for you. Know your limits, and don't compromise on them one inch.

KEEP YOUR STRATEGY SIMPLE

Once you wrap your mind around what you want to do with an online business and how it might fit into your lifestyle, you can set up a strategy. What separates the passive earners from the wannabe dreamers when it comes to making the internet work for you? First, consider an overall strategic point. With any innovation, there is a cycle of interest that goes through several phases. For example, when motion pictures first became available early in the 20th century, audiences were entranced simply by watching a horse run on the screen. But things quickly got more complicated. People wanted to see stories, and they wanted to see movie stars. They also wanted to see color photography. As soon as color pictures appeared, black and white seemed like ancient history. In the same way, when the internet first started it was amazing that it existed at all. Emailing and instant messaging seemed like miracles. But the same thing happened to the internet that took place with motion pictures, and in a much shorter time. The technology that seemed so remarkable at first was quickly taken for granted. In other words, your strategy needs to be ever-evolving, and you must be ready to change your approach on a dime.

What can you learn from this in terms of building passive income on the internet? Does it mean you need to build an elaborate website with all the bells and whistles to attract attention? At first glance, that might seem to make sense. After all, if people want excitement, shouldn't you try to give it to them?

The answer is no—for two reasons. First, unless you have an unlimited budget, you will never be able to build a website that excites your audience simply from a technological perspective. By now, you've just seen too many websites to be thrilled by another one. So this is a situation where the "less is more" rule definitely applies. As you begin to explore making money online, you've got to prioritize minimizing the technical issues. You also need to minimize the costs—first because cutting expenses is usually a good idea, but also because putting money into website technology just doesn't bring returns. There are many ways that you can build a blog or landing page that will completely fulfill your needs using platforms like Squarespace, WordPress, and other easy-to-use sites that will also fill the needs of your potential customers.

IDENTIFY YOUR CUSTOMERS

Now you're ready to start identifying exactly who those customers are. We're going identify them using three different categories—an objective measure, a subjective measure, and a third classification that we'll call "ECB," or expected customer behavior. Let's look at these three categories in order.

Objective Measure

Basically, the objective measure refers to anything you can say about your customers through numbers. For example, are you able to determine what age groups are most interested in what you have to offer? If you return to the old-time baseball concept for a moment, think about what demographic might form most of your website's viewership. You can find out how many people have visited websites devoted to your interest. You can also find out how many people have done web searches for phrases like "early baseball" or "history of sports." But that kind of research is usually not effective in terms of cost and time.

Chances are, you yourself are probably your best source of objective information about a specific interest. Most of the people who share your interest are probably much like you. That's especially true if you've found a specific interest. There may be millions of people who follow NFL football, but a lot fewer are interested in what baseball was like a hundred years ago. And remember that can work to your advantage. Even if there are only a thousand people in the whole country who share your interest, if you can get them all to send you $10 a month to subscribe to a newsletter about your topic, then you've got a significant amount of passive income.

Subjective Measure

Subjective measures of your potential customers are those that aren't expressed simply in numbers. They're generally understood anecdotally or in combination with a numerical analysis. For example, during presidential election debates, almost every candidate for the past 30 years has worn a red tie. It's just something that voters want to see, and it goes beyond objective categories of age, income, or geographical location. Focus groups show that both men and women respond more positively to someone in a red tie rather than a blue one. It's just a gut feeling that people have. It's totally subjective. But it's a fact, so why fight it? That's why you'll see so many red ties on the debate stage.

It's important to be aware of the subjective issues of your potential customers. For instance, in every field of interest there are certain phrases, certain names, and certain ideas by which people recognize each other. We can call it jargon, although that word may have a negative connotation. It's really just a set of beliefs that a group of people shares, and that provides the starting point for a possible relationship. If you want to bond with someone who likes motorcycles, for example, you might want to mention the classic Indian brand of motorcycle that was popular in the 1940s. As soon as you bring that up, a motorcycle enthusiast will know that you have a certain level of interest. But if he or she mentions the Indian motorcycle and you have no idea what it is, it's clear that your interest is less deep. So think about what those subjective touchstones might be for your potential customers, and make sure that you put them to use.

Expected Customer Behavior

The final element in you customer profile concerns the beliefs that a customer has of you, your website, and any product or service you will provide. This final element also includes the beliefs you have about your customers. All of this can be referred to as *expected customer behavior* (ECB). And regardless of what kind of an online passive income business you intend to create, you can likely count on at least one of three things to ring true.

First, if you expect anyone to pay you $100 or more through your website for something that is not a tangible product, that expectation is very misplaced. Online customers just aren't going to do it. But there's another side to this coin: online customers also expect that you *will*, in fact, ask them to spend $100 or more—so if you refute that expectation by asking for less, you have a good chance of making a sale.

Secondly, if you labor over your website or blog in the expectation that visitors will explore every corner of it, you will be disappointed. Even if web visitors are passionate about a particular topic, the vast majority of people stay on a site for less than five minutes, and often less than one minute. That's another reason why a simple, well-organized website is better than a more elaborate one. So, put your best information up front, show the visitor what you have to offer, and make responding to that offer as quick and easy as possible. That's definitely the most efficient route for building a passive income stream.

Finally—although it's true that elaborate websites are a mistake—there is one aspect of a website that you need to take very seriously. You must update your website as often as possible. Ideally this should be done every day, or every two days at the outset. This is probably the single most important fact you need to know about a website business of any kind. Visitors quickly learn how often a site is updated, and they will return accordingly. That's another reason why blogs are so much better than more complicated sites. It's easy to update a blog on a daily basis. The few minutes you spend updating your site are the absolutely essential foundation for building passive income on the web. This is especially true with one online passive income model in particular: ecommerce.

UNLOCKING THE POWER OF ECOMMERCE

Generating passive income online can be done in many ways, from selling services and freelancing to offering a couple of simple digital products in conjunction with your blog or interest-based page. Now let's dig in a little deeper and talk about the big fish of the online business world—ecommerce.

While any online selling of a product or service can be considered ecommerce, for our purposes here, we are using the term to refer to a larger dedicated effort to sell physical products online. And while this particular model requires a more complicated setup, it will bear fruit in the long term for your passive income lifestyle.

With ecommerce, you will be selling physical products directly, even if the products you are selling are not yours. You won't be driving customers to someone else's landing page or website. You'll be selling products from a platform of your choice. Whether you're the one who fulfills the order and ships it to your customers depends on which model you choose. Regardless of the platform you choose to sell from or your fulfillment arrangement, you are selling the items directly to the consumer and reaping the profits. Those buyers are your customers.

WHY ECOMMERCE?

As you move through the decision-making process, consider the pros and cons of ecommerce. Weigh these carefully before you jump into the ecommerce fray. First, the pros:

- *No need for a physical store.* Sometimes for real-world retailers, needing a physical location is the biggest hurdle.
- *Flexible hours.* You can make sales 24/7. The internet never sleeps.
- *Low overhead.* Because many of the processes in an ecommerce business are automated, it requires less staff to run your business than a traditional retail store.
- *No geographical limitations.* Business owners can sell on a global level with relative ease.
- *Familiar shopping model.* Unless you're living under a rock, everyone knows what online shopping is. You don't have to educate your audience that you exist.

Next, keep the cons in mind. They include:

- *Inventory.* Ecommerce businesses require inventory. If you're drop-shipping, this may not fall on your shoulders, but products need to be stored somewhere.
- *Price matching.* Brick-and-mortar stores have price-matching programs that will give their shoppers the online price, thus beating you in the pricing game. Not only are brick-and-mortars able to match your online price for the customer, they are also able to deliver immediately, allowing the buyer to have their item as soon as possible.
- *Lack of instant gratification.* Consumers don't receive your product until it arrives at their door days later. This sometimes makes them feel empty-handed for some time after making an online purchase.
- *Chargebacks.* Credit cards can be quite liberal when it comes to approving chargebacks for consumers. In my experience, credit card companies favor the consumer far more than the sellers.
- *Good, old-fashioned competition.* Ecommerce is a popular business model (that's why we're writing about it!), so you will find you have *a lot* of competition.

Think on these before you commit to an online ecommerce model. If you feel that your choice has taken all of the pros and cons into consideration, it's time to start thinking about storefronts.

When the average person thinks about having a business online, most of the time what they picture probably falls into the ecommerce realm. They think of online stores and platforms where they can shop and buy something they are looking for. Because shopping online is now such a commonly understood concept, it can be wildly profitable. It has a lot of moving parts and there can be a lot to manage, but at least you don't have to start out educating the public that shopping online is even an option. You will not be a pioneer; instead you are walking into a lucrative and established model. That means you will have plenty of options at your disposal.

THE BIG FIVE

There are five common reasons why choosing ecommerce is a strong passive income plan:

1. *There is a higher barrier to entry.* Because of this, many people choosing a business model get intimidated and choose other models with lower barriers to entry. That leaves more room for you.

2. *There is more work upfront.* The work of laying a proper foundation takes place upfront, which may scare some people off, thus opening the door for you to dominate that space. After that, the main focus tends to be on driving traffic, optimizing for conversions, and providing an excellent customer experience.

3. *A high percentage of your competitors are mom-and-pop businesses.* There are not a ton of sophisticated players in the markets doing less than $1 million in revenue. This makes it much easier to dominate.

4. *Selling physical products online does not require a lot of persuasion techniques.* If people go to a website to buy a dog bowl, it doesn't take a lot of psychology to close the sale.

5. *You enjoy a higher-than-average dollar-per-visitor value.* Given the fact that people come to your website to buy a specific item and you don't have to do a lot to persuade them to buy it, the conversion rates, on average, are high with ecommerce.

SOLO WEBSITE VS. MULTI-VENDOR STOREFRONT

There are some great multi-vendor storefronts you can use as opposed to going the solo ecommerce route. You might ask why you would create your own ecommerce store when you can sell from one of the online giants like Amazon, Etsy, and eBay, which already have substantial credibility and millions of shoppers. Both the solo and the multi-vendor storefront routes are viable options, but stand-alone online stores offer you some benefits that simply can't be found on a bigger site.

Benefits of Being a Stand-Alone Ecommerce Store

It is awesome when your products are featured in an active, thriving marketplace like Amazon or eBay. However, there are some benefits to being a stand-alone ecommerce store. Here are a few that are commonly appreciated:

- *Full control.* When you are solo, you maintain full control of your business. You can sell what you want and how you want. You don't have additional compliance regulations or restrictions beyond the standard ones any online store would have to be aware of.
- *No sharing of customers.* Your customers are yours. You get every bit of data they are willing to give you, including their name, email address, phone number, address, and permission to contact them. No one else gets to have your clients or tell you how you can and cannot communicate with them, or whether you can sell more items to them.
- *More profit.* You are not sharing the profit from your sales with any other organizations like you will on platforms like Amazon, Etsy, and eBay.
- *Brand clarity.* When you're on a major site, someone may purchase from you because you sell an item they were searching for. But the impression that sticks with them is that they bought the item on Amazon. When someone buys from your own ecommerce site, the only association they can attach to the item is your brand, because there aren't any other vendors or brands selling on your website.

Whether your ecommerce site is an extension of a business you already have or an independent site, understanding your options will help you pick the best route for you, your business, and your unique situation. The biggest benefit by far of the solo route is your ability to maintain maximum control of your business, the direction it goes, and the factors that impact your success.

TYPES OF ECOMMERCE

There are several types of ecommerce business models to choose from. Since this book focuses on passive models that can easily get up and running quickly, we are going to explore only three of the many options: drop-shipping, wholesaling and warehousing, and white labeling and manufacturing.

It is no accident that the three options are listed in that order. Why? Because they are listed in order of complexity. If you are getting started in ecommerce for the first time and are looking to start with the easiest model, start with drop-shipping.

Drop-Shipping

Drop-shipping is when you sell items on your website that are manufactured, fulfilled, and shipped to your customers by someone else. Generally these relationships are established between you and a manufacturer or a wholesaler who has a warehouse full of the items you would like to sell. Once the proper agreements are in place, the manufacturer or wholesaler will send you images of the products you wish to sell along with pricing. You will then place those items for sale in your ecommerce store. Your job is to sell the items, and the manufacturer or wholesaler will fulfill the orders and ship them to your customers.

One of the benefits people love most about the drop-shipping model is that there is very little upfront investment. You don't buy any of the products until one is ordered from you and paid for. Once your foundation is set up with a selling platform, and your relationship with your drop-shipping partner is in place, your primary focus is driving targeted buyers to your store and providing an amazing customer experience. Once the sale is made, that is when you pull money out of your pocket to pay for the item sold. This is a low-risk, high-reward model. You don't have to stock any inventory or deal with the headache of order fulfillment.

Some of the drawbacks are that you have no control over the shipping and fulfillment and sometimes your suppliers let you down. If a supplier is running behind or forgets to provide you with a tracking number, that increases your customer service responsibilities. Also, since you're not keeping any of the inventory, you don't always know if an item is running low. You could end up unknowingly selling something that is out of stock. Then you have to deal with the customer service and reputation ramifications.

The good news is that if you don't feel the supplier you have chosen is living up to your standards, it is pretty easy to get out of a drop-shipping contract. Your assets are entirely digital. It's much easier to transition an ecommerce business that uses drop-shipping as its fulfillment model than it is if you have a warehouse full of items that have already been manufactured for you.

Wholesaling and Warehousing

This model involves buying products in bulk and storing them in a warehouse somewhere. Usually people who prefer this model are selling product in volume. People most commonly use this in a business-to-business (B2B) market as opposed to a business-to-consumer (B2C) model.

With this model, you get better pricing because you're buying in bulk instead of making one-off purchases, as in a drop-shipping business. If you're buying in bulk and selling the items individually on your website to consumers, you also have better margins than you do with drop-shipping.

However, if you're like most people using this model, which has lower margins, you are selling in bulk to businesses who are selling to consumers. In most wholesale businesses, you need to create enough sales volume to make up for the smaller margins. This model also requires high upfront investments for purchasing and housing the product.

White Labeling and Manufacturing

Manufacturing is when you pay to have the items created for you. In white labeling, you aren't manufacturing the product, but your licensing contract allows you to put your name or brand on it as if you are the manufacturer. With this scenario, you are either manufacturing products overseas or importing them from overseas and putting your brand on them. You are the top of the product chain at this point.

When you are importing or manufacturing overseas, your margins are much higher. You get to create the product for a lower price, then sell it online for a much higher price. You also control all the shipping and fulfillment yourself. While this is more work, it has a lot of benefits, too. You get to control the entire cycle and always know what's going on with the product. Also, at this point, you can take advantage of wholesalers and drop-shippers to retail your products for you.

This model is not for the commitment-phobe. There is no easy way to end a manufacturing contract. You had the products made, you've imported them into your country, and you have them sitting in a warehouse somewhere. You also have to develop a process to monitor and maintain quality control. This is definitely an advanced model for earning passive income online. There is almost always a large cash investment required upfront, so you need to have a financial plan.

ECOMMERCE PLATFORMS

Regardless of which ecommerce business model you choose to go with, you have to create an online storefront You have three options for independent sites: a custom website, hosted solutions, and self-hosted solutions. Which platform is right for you depends on your situation, knowledge, and finances.

Custom Website

While you can build your own ecommerce website from the ground up, why would you? Even if you have the capital, resources, and intelligence, you would be hard-pressed to believe that yours would be better than one of the many solutions already out there.

Hosted Solutions

These are often referred to as "hosting for ecommerce," but it's not just a hosting service. Ecommerce-hosted solutions are considered *software as a service* (SaaS) because they are designed to be ecommerce stores in a box. We hesitate to say that a hosted solution has everything you need as a store owner, but if it doesn't, it will come pretty close.

Unless you're already an ecommerce expert, it can take quite a while before you know enough to optimize your store for the highest results. By going with a hosted solution, a lot of the heavy lifting is done for you.

Here are some top reasons for choosing a hosted solution:

- *Better security.* Hosted solutions would go out of business quickly if they weren't able to protect the stores using their platforms. Therefore, they tend to have decent security built in.
- *Backup systems.* Backup and data recovery are usually included as part of what you get with a hosted solution.
- *Hands-off maintenance and upgrades.* When you go with a hosted solution, maintaining the technology behind your storefront is not your responsibility. If they want to remain competitive, they will strive to continually upgrade the features that benefit you.
- *Quick and easy installation.* Hosted solutions are meant to have a turnkey feel to them, so installation is generally a nonissue.
- *Support.* Hosted solutions will come with support; most of the time you get unlimited access.

You're entering this game at the right time. When the first generation of hosted and nonhosted solutions came to market, they made a lot of mistakes. The good news is that the newest wave of them learned from those mistakes. Remember, all platforms have their pros and cons, so it's important to do your due diligence and find the solution that works for you. Three of the heavy hitters in this area are BigCommerce, Shopify, and Volusion.

BigCommerce (www.bigcommerce.com) is the preferred platform choice of Ezra Firestone, one of the leading experts in ecommerce strategy. That is a pretty heavy endorsement all by itself. But here are a few more benefits that make this platform an excellent choice:

- Affordable pricing starting at $29.95 for almost every feature and capping out at $249.95 per month for a Pro plan
- Google Trusted Stores certification assistance
- Assisted setup to increase sales
- Easy to integrate with eBay, Google Shopping, and more
- Excellent customer service
- Real-time quotes, gift cards, and 24/7 phone/email/chat support included in the base plan
- Popular with small- to medium-size web stores
- Unlimited products, storage, and bandwidth

Shopify (www.shopify.com) has some great things going for it, including:

- Affordable plans starting at $29 per month and capping at the $299 Advanced Shopify plan
- Popular with small web stores
- Innovative app store to expand your default web store
- Unlimited products and bandwidth
- Easy to integrate with shipping carriers, fulfillment centers, and drop-shipping companies
- Manage store and payments via a mobile app
- Point-of-sale option to take payments in person
- Assistance in setting up your store

Volusion (www.volusion.com) is another great option, featuring:

- Affordable plans starting at $29 per month
- Popular among all business sizes
- Abandoned cart recovery services at the cheapest price point
- Built-in loyalty program
- Built-in deal-of-the-day option
- eBay and Amazon integration

Self-Hosted Solutions

Self-hosted solutions are a good option if you are not quite tech-savvy enough to build your own website but still want the convenience of having the built-in core features ecommerce businesses care about. Self-hosted solutions trade convenience for full control and customization capabilities. They do not fall into the SaaS category. Think of it more like a customized shopping cart with some special features that cater to ecommerce.

Self-hosted solutions focus on the basic functionality that matters to ecommerce sites. Some of this functionality includes:

- Catalog features
- Shopping cart
- Checkout flow

They may not have all the bells and whistles of a fully hosted solution, but the basics are covered, and you can enjoy the ability to customize your store on your own. There isn't really a wrong answer; it's all about preference and what's right for your specific situation.

If having the ability to fully customize the look and feel of your web store is important to you and you really want to build your own site, try a self-hosted solution. That way you have some basic functionality to work with and you can still make the changes that are most important to you.

Here are a couple of self-hosted solutions to consider:

1. *WooCommerce* (www.woocommerce.com). Its features include:
   - Free to download
   - Runs on WordPress
   - Light application that does not tax your server
   - Above average basic functionality with hundreds of plug-ins to enhance it
   - Makes use of most free and paid WordPress plug-ins
   - Easy to set up and customize
   - Easy to navigate if you're already familiar with WordPress

❧ Huge library of gorgeous themes available for affordable prices

This is a wonderful choice if you plan to link an ecommerce portal to your blog. So in the case of the example we used earlier about starting an online community dedicated to old-time baseball, you could write a blog on a site like WordPress, then sell books or memorabilia using WooCommerce.

2. *Magento* (http://magento.com). Magneto's many features include:
   - ❧ Free download of community edition
   - ❧ Boasts that 11 percent of the market uses it
   - ❧ Most integration options in the industry
   - ❧ Hundreds of high-quality templates to choose from
   - ❧ No need to upgrade to a better solution in the future
   - ❧ Can easily set up different storefronts with one shared product base
   - ❧ Feature heavy

Magento has the most bells and whistles in the self-hosted solutions world, but it is also a beast on your server. Once you're large enough, it's commonly suggested you host your back end on a separate server.

ADDITIONAL CONSIDERATIONS

Remember, even with hosted solutions or self-hosted solutions, you will still have some important aspects you will need to take care of before your web store is complete.

Payment Solution

You will still need to set up a way to take money. This can be as simple as using PayPal, or you can apply for your own merchant account. While all the solutions mentioned above come with shopping carts, they don't come with a payment processing solution. As you'll read in Chapter 4, you still need to set up a way to take money.

Analytics

Most platforms likely have integration options to make this easy, but if you want to track your results and see how your web traffic is performing, you will need to hook your ecommerce site up to analytics.

Images and Design

Depending on what you want to do, you may still have need of some design work to make your web store complete. It's possible you may be able to get by without this, but it's something to keep in mind.

Content

Every website needs content. Whether you write it yourself or hire a ghostwriter, one way or the other you need to factor this into your process.

GET THE LAY OF THE LAND

You don't have to reinvent the wheel when you are trying to research potential ecommerce markets. Go to popular websites like Etsy and eBay and look at the different categories and subcategories listed. Type your target keywords into Google and look at the top-ranking sites. How do they categorize their products and websites? Sites like Amazon and eBay aren't casually organized—there is a purpose behind the way they are structured. This also shows you how the prospects in this market are used to finding the products they are looking for.

When doing market research for a new ecommerce business, there are a couple of tools that will help you. First is WatchCount.com (www.watchcount.com). There, you can type in your keywords and see the most-sold items on eBay. You can also search by categories to see the top-selling offers per category. Another great place to look is Internet Retailer (www.digitalcommerce360.com/internet-retailer/). This is a useful resource for anyone in the ecommerce space.

PARTING THOUGHTS

As you can see, the only limit to how you can make money online is your own imagination. In this chapter, you've read about how to get your thinking straight so you can start to plan your online strategy. Once you assess your goals in relation to your interests and skill set, you can make the moves toward turning your online vision into reality. The example we used in this chapter—the ecommerce model—is perhaps the most common method of earning online income, and for good reason. It can be as big or as small of a site as you want, you can focus on selling physical or digital products, and you can automate many of the functions. It's a viable, versatile way to get money pouring into your online revenue bucket.

In the next chapter, we're going to take a deeper dive and talk you through some ways to maximize your ability to earn passive income online by tweaking your processes, focusing on your customer, and partnering with other businesses to earn affiliate income.

CHAPTER FOUR

LEVELING UP YOUR ONLINE STRATEGY

Now that you've done some initial research and wrapped your mind around the concept of your online passive income site, it's time to dig in deeper and put your plan into action. In this chapter, you'll learn more about creating passive income on the internet and hear from creative entrepreneurs who have done just that. With them, you'll see firsthand the challenges and opportunities of internet business. And one of the biggest lessons? As in any other business, you've still got to put the customer first.

PRIORITIZE POS QUALITY

The customer experience is paramount to online sales success, whether you're selling online courses, webinars, or hard products like jewelry or handmade items. If a customer has a poor experience during their buying process, you've lost them—and probably for good. Jane's story is a good example of how making that connection between a strong customer experience at the point of sale (POS) and securing a repeat customer for the long-term is key to your success with an online passive income model. Here is Jane's story, in her own words:

I decided to start an online jewelry business. I already had my own line of inexpensive but sophisticated jewelry. I had rings, earrings, and necklaces. These were pieces I'd developed over a period of years. I was confident that there were large numbers of buyers for them— but until that point, I had only sold at art fairs and flea markets. I knew the internet was going to be a very different game. I knew everything about my product, but I knew almost nothing about the electronic marketplace.

So, I got a few books about website design and internet marketing. They were useful, but what really helped was understanding my own likes and dislikes when I make a purchase. In thinking about it, I was surprised that I basically looked for the same things when I bought online or when at a traditional brick-and-mortar store.

For instance, I really dislike waiting in line. I may spend some time walking around a store to find something I like, but once I've found it, I want to complete the purchase as quickly as possible. That means I don't want to wait very long for a salesperson to check me out, and I really don't want to run into some sort of technical glitch. Even in really big stores, it's amazing how often I'll hear, "The computer is down." When that happens, it's just a chance for me to change my mind about even making the purchase in the first place, and I'm sure other people feel the same way.

I realized that I felt the same way about shopping online, but even more so. It seems like everything gets compressed on the internet. You want it all to move very quickly. You might spend 20 to 30 minutes wandering around a store, but the average time on a website is a tiny fraction of that. People just want it to happen really fast and efficiently.

When it doesn't happen that way—especially when they're actually completing the purchase—they don't just get annoyed. They actually get scared. They worry about what's going on with their money. If they've used a credit card (which most people are going to do) and the whole buying process suddenly gets stalled, they don't know what to do. They're wondering if they should click on the "submit" button again, but they're also afraid they might get double billed. You don't want that sort of thing to happen if you intend to develop repeat business—and repeat business is the absolute foundation of passive income on the internet. And what you really don't want is for the buyer to do something that's much easier than walking out of a store. You don't want them to click "cancel" with their mouse and exit the website. If that happens, you've lost a sale, and you can also be sure they're never coming back to your site.

Jane's story raises a key principle. In an earlier chapter, you read that less is sometimes more when it comes to setting up an online income stream. Try to keep your site as clean and simple as possible— and make this especially true of the payment process. More than half of all buyers cancel at the last minute, during the final process of entering their personal information and receiving approval. That 50 percent figure goes even higher if you ask for any additional information. Most often, people disconnect because of the slowness of the process. If they've gotten this far, they want to buy your product, but they're frustrated. So you've got to make it easy for them. Let's look at a few ways you can do that.

Use a Payment System

You don't want to spend your free time processing payments and dealing with billing issues. This is supposed to be passive income, after all! So find a company to outsource that function, too, like Square or Stripe. You can easily link your site to a payment service that will process the billing. Many such services are available, and it shouldn't be hard to find one that's right for you. Think about online purchases that you've made that have gone smoothly—especially when the billing has been outsourced to a payment service—then contact the website and get a referral. This should be no problem, especially if you identify yourself as a satisfied customer. You might even be able to create a linking relationship with that site in which you promote their site while they, in turn, promote yours.

Build Confidence by Sharing Safety, Shipping, and Returns Information

If you choose to handle credit card payments yourself rather than through a payment service, be sure to include some text about the security of a purchase. By federal law, customers have the right to dispute credit card charges if they don't get what they were promised. They can also dispute any unauthorized charges that appear on their credit cards—all of which have zero liability policies. That means card holders pay nothing for unauthorized use. Federal law requires online orders to be shipped by the date promised. If no delivery time was stated, the order has to be shipped within 30 days. Late shipment means customers can cancel the order and get a refund. They also have the right to reject merchandise if it's defective or was misrepresented. Make this safety information available to your customers. It builds confidence in your business.

Speaking of inspiring confidence, you'll want to be sure that you set clear terms for shipping and returns for physical products and satisfaction guarantees if you are delivering online products like courses, webinars, or ebooks.

For physical products, free shipping is a big draw. Many of the most successful web businesses offer free delivery with orders above a certain amount. But this doesn't mean that the delivery is really free. You can and should build the delivery cost into your price—but now you can use the powerful word "free" in your offer. And you'll be surprised by the number of people who increase their orders so that they can get free delivery. As for content products that are delivered online, the word "instant" is key. You will want to set up your site so that it delivers any online content you sell as soon as the customer's payment is processed. This is a function you can easily automate through the online payment tool or white label store support you sync with your site.

A "no questions asked" return policy for physical goods and a money-back guarantee for e-content is also a good idea, and you should feature this prominently on your site. Once again, this is a real confidence builder—and the fact is, very few people actually return a purchase if you give them what they expect to receive. Once or twice a year you may have to eat a return that may not be legitimate—but as a cost of doing business, it's definitely worthwhile. In fact, one of the best ways to build goodwill is to treat someone well when they make a return. Very often you'll quickly get a new order from that same customer.

Discount Your Way to Customer Loyalty

As you build relationships with customers, the goal is to keep them coming back to your site for more. One great way to do that is to offer discount coupons for return customers. Once you've gotten a buyer's email address, you can set up an automated email marketing program that reaches out to them regularly with information on how they can get a lower price on their next purchase, or notifications of new products or services. There are several options for programs that will help you automate your email marketing function, including (but most certainly not limited to):

- ⊷ Mailchimp
- ⊷ HubSpot
- ⊷ Constant Contact
- ⊷ Infusionsoft
- ⊷ GetResponse
- ⊷ Pardot

⃰† Campaign Monitor

⃰† SendinBlue

⃰† Campaigner

⃰† Zoho Campaigns

Make these offers time sensitive. That means the order has to be placed by a certain date or the discount will expire. At the time of their initial purchase, be sure to alert your customers that they'll be getting these discount offers in the future as they are opting in by sharing their email address. This will make it less likely they'll treat your emails as spam.

A good way to present discount coupons is in an email that you send to confirm a first order. This is a chance to start building long-term relationships with your customers. After all, the buyer has just sent you money for the first time. Even with all your assurances and protections there's bound to be a little uncertainty. Don't ignore that. Thank them for their order, and thank them for their trust. Use that specific word. Then include the discount coupon code, a number they can enter with their next purchase. And finally, make sure that you fill the order promptly and completely.

KNOW YOUR LANE AND STAY IN IT

The online jewelry business you read about in the previous section can be very successful, but in terms of passive income it may not be the ideal enterprise for everyone. That's because of the fulfillment issues that simply can't be avoided. For example, the purchases will need to be inventoried, boxed, shipped, and possibly insured. It can get complicated. If dealing with those issues is not how you envision spending your passive income career, then make the call now before you get in too deep and realize it's not for you. There are other ways to sell things online. For example, if you don't want the hassle of dealing with physical products, steer your business plan in the direction of products or services that can be instantly delivered online—most of which fall under the umbrella of intellectual property (which you'll read more about in Chapter 9). From marketing assets and content products like ebooks to webinars and courses, there are endless possibilities for what you can sell online without dealing with inventory. And if such products fit well into the purpose of your online business, you've got endless earning potential. Knowing that you have marketable ideas you can turn into profit is the first step; acting on it is the key. Take Michael's story as an example of a "knowing your lane" success story:

I always liked to take wildlife photos, but I never gave it much attention. Part of the reason was the cost and also because of the time that was involved. In the old days before everything went digital, there was the cost of the camera, the cost of the film, and the cost of the developing process. All those costs had to be paid before you even had anything to look at. Now, with the dominance of digital photography imbedded in our culture (everyone has a camera if they have a smart phone, after all), making a living selling photos is a no-brainer, low-stress option.

For me, digital photography was a really wonderful innovation both personally and professionally. On a personal level, I had always been interested in taking pictures and now the hassle factor was hugely reduced. And from a business perspective, I realized that digital pictures were the ideal product to market on the internet. That's because the delivery process was entirely electronic. Buyers could see the images I had for sale, pay for them with a credit card, and then download them instantly.

At first, I was amazed at how simple it was. I was able to build and maintain a functional website for about $50 a month. I also had no trouble setting up credit card payments. I had some interesting wildlife photos that I had taken in Yellowstone, and I offered them for sale on my website for a few dollars each. Once again, there was a pleasant surprise. It only took a few days to make my first sale. When that happened, I really felt like I had stumbled upon a moneymaking machine capable of creating multiple streams of passive income. For me, the problem was that I didn't really know how to keep the momentum going through smart marketing yet. After making three *small sales in the first week my site was up, I didn't make another sale for more than a month. I had more to learn than I thought.*

Michael's story shows that latching onto a way to market your personal interest or skill to other people is a great jumping-off point for creating a passive revenue stream. However, the idea alone isn't the gold mine—it's all in the way you sell it. There are several important points you can learn from Michael's story. First, if you want to create passive income very quickly, internet marketing of intellectual property has many advantages. You can avoid all the issues of creating and shipping a physical object such as a piece of jewelry. And whether you realize it or not, you almost certainly have the raw material for creating intellectual property right now. Everyone has a story to tell— so it's just a matter of putting your story into a marketable format. There are people who have written about how they got out of debt, for example—and there are even people who have written about how they got *into* debt. If you're a parent, you can tell what you've learned from raising your children. You can write about fly-fishing or firefighting, cooking or carpet cleaning. You can even write about writing—and if you can't write, it's easy to hire someone who will write for you. If you have a story, it's a story you can market.

BUILDING YOUR SITE

As you're getting started, don't be intimidated by the technical aspects of building your site. You don't have to be a computer genius to have a perfectly good website. A quick Google search will give you many sites for website creation, which include the ability to accept credit card payments or, as you read in the last chapter, you can create an easy-to-manage ecommerce store with the help of white label sites.

That's the good news—but there's also the other news, which is that no matter how slick your site looks, slick alone doesn't sell. You've got to put in the work on the back end to ensure that the customer's experience keeps them coming back for more. After all, you are banking on this income stream to be successful enough to run in the background of your life. If you always have to chase down new customers because you only get "one and done" sales, then something is missing in your success formula. And that something is most likely rooted in the design, ethos, and functionality of your site. Remember, Michael had a great idea and a solid product. Yet his sales flattened. After some initial success, he encountered a dry spell—with no sales and a diminishing number of visitors to his site. Why did that happen? And why does it continue happening to web entrepreneurs, even when things seem to go well at the beginning?

In short, Michael planned to fail by failing to plan. But you can avoid the fate of empty virtual shopping carts by making a few smart moves at the beginning of your website planning process so you can consistently and continually generate passive income. Quite simply, these are the moves you need to make. They don't cost a lot of money, but they do require a commitment on your part. You need to commit some time, and you need to commit yourself to learning what you need to know. By making that effort at the beginning, your biggest task in the future will be keeping track of the money that's coming into your site.

Being Shallow Is a Good Thing

Essentially, any business is a system for serving the needs of clients or customers. A website business is a system for serving those needs with the amazing speed and efficiency that technology has made possible. Regardless of what physical product or intellectual property you're selling, here's the first thing you need to understand: People want things to happen fast on the internet. You're selling instant gratification, and you've got to provide that before anything else.

The buzzword for this in the online business world is "shallow." The *shallowness* of your site refers to the number of clicks that are needed to perform a certain function. The fewer the clicks, the shallower your site will be. Keeping your site shallow is extremely important, especially in the buying function. Earlier we mentioned how customers dislike waiting in line in retail stores. Well, they really don't like waiting on the internet, either. So, when you select a program for building your website, make sure that the checkout process is as quick and efficient as possible.

Roll Out the Welcome Mat with Good Design

Assuming your site operates quickly and correctly, what else do customers like on a commercial website? People want to feel some energy from the site. They like to see pictures. They like to see color. They like to see graphics that are creative without being overwhelming. If you've done a good job of setting up your site, providing these enhancements will cost you next to nothing.

What nobody likes on a website is a lot of text in a bland format. Online customers usually don't make a purchase on their first website visit, but they'll come back if the visit was good, which means they found it interesting, entertaining, and quality-driven. A good visit means more seeing rather than reading. Good is wanting to see everything that's on your site today and wanting to come back tomorrow to see more.

Update Consistently with Creative Content

This is a really crucial point. Potential buyers will come back to your site if their first visit was good—but what will they want the second time? They'll want it to be good again, but they'll also want it to be different. They won't want to see the same thing all over again. So you've got to continuously update your website. In fact, *continuously* isn't a strong enough word. You've got to *constantly* update your site. Nothing is worse than a site whose last update was three months ago—and it's amazing how often that happens! If customers feel like you've ignored the upkeep of your site, they'll suspect you might ignore them also. When that happens, they click away to something else. So, keep your site up to date.

There are two very easy ways to make sure your site always has something new. The first is to add a website forum, which is an area for customers to provide comments and feedback. Be sure that your site builder program includes the ability to add a forum. You may find that the same two or three people account for most of the comments, but that doesn't mean that more people aren't reading them. As customers become used to buying online, they feel at home using forums and they exchange information freely. So this is a great way to build a sense of community into your site.

Another easy way to keep your site current is by adding a blog. This will also let you bring some of your own personality into the site. It will give visitors the sense that they're doing business with a human being and not just a machine. The word *blog* is actually a contraction of "web log"—meaning a diary or journal that appears on an internet website. Right now there are millions and millions of blogs, and some of them are hugely influential—politically, culturally, and commercially. As a web entrepreneur, having a blog on your site is an opportunity to do some really valuable things. It lets you bring your personality into your business and to give it your own a flesh and blood identity. Creating a blog for your site doesn't have to take a lot of time. Sometimes an entry can be just a link to an interesting newspaper article or website you discovered.

Beyond what you're selling and how you sell it, blogs and forums provide value-added content for your site. Marketing jewelry, books, or nature photos can be your front end, and you should provide excellent value and customer service there. But you'll sell a lot more of your product if people come to your site even when they don't need to buy a cookbook.

Maximize Your In-Site Marketing

Once you get into a rhythm with your website design, there are lots of other options you can explore. You can plan to offer subscriptions to a weekly or monthly email newsletter, for example—or you can create a members' area on your site with discount coupons and other benefits. When you make the effort to add value to your site, people will start coming just for that value—but all those people will become buyers in a very short time. Besides creating passive income, a web business is a chance to create real online relationships. Your website can express

STEPS TO A SUCCESSFUL WEB BUSINESS

If you expect to get much of your revenue through your website, you'll need to consider these seven steps for successful ecommerce businesses, according to Allen Moon, founder of On Deck Marketing.

1. *Find a need and fill it.* Look for a market first, not a product. If your business will be primarily online, look to online forums and social media to figure out the problem you're solving and how to best position it.

2. *Write copy that sells.* Find compelling and enticing ways to draw people in. Create urgency and appeal to bring people through the sales process.

3. *Design and build an easy-to-use website.* If it's not simple, expect potential customers to abandon their purchase before they hit "buy." Don't go overboard with fancy interfaces that take too long to load or complex purchase systems to pay.

4. *Use search engines to drive traffic to your site.* Consider pay-per-click-style advertising to start.

5. *Establish an expert reputation for yourself.* Give away free expert content. Create articles, videos, or any other content that people will find useful. Distribute that content through online article directories or social media sites like Facebook, Reddit, or LinkedIn—or even your local chamber of commerce or Rotary Club.

6. *Follow up with your customers and subscribers with email.* Build an opt-in list so you can email customers with new products and offers.

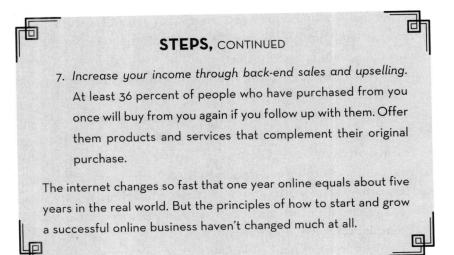

STEPS, CONTINUED

7. *Increase your income through back-end sales and upselling.*
   At least 36 percent of people who have purchased from you
   once will buy from you again if you follow up with them. Offer
   them products and services that complement their original
   purchase.

The internet changes so fast that one year online equals about five
years in the real world. But the principles of how to start and grow
a successful online business haven't changed much at all.

your personality and your creativity as well as sell your product.
Making this happen is really the fun part of internet commerce. But
first, you have to build an audience.

IF YOU BUILD IT, WILL THEY COME?

The number of websites is well over the multimillion mark with the
potential of crossing into the billions. According to the *2017 Domain
Name Industry Brief*, published by VeriSign, the internet boasted more
than 332.4 million domain names by the end of 2017. With millions
of websites out there, getting visitors to your individual site is often
the biggest challenge. Your strategies for doing so may include search
engines, paid search services, and affiliates. Let's consider them one at
a time.

Search Engines

Search engines have become a ubiquitous part of American culture.
Every day millions of Americans go online to search the internet or
"Google" something or someone. According to a 2016 report from the
Pew Internet & American Life project—which produces reports that
explore the impact of the internet—79 percent of Americans say they

make purchases online, and 82 percent say they at least sometimes read online customer ratings or reviews before purchasing items for the first time. Web searching is the primary point of discovery for most of us, especially when we are seeking new products or services. So how do you get noticed?

Perhaps the most important—and inexpensive—strategy in getting people to your website is to rank high for your preferred keywords on the main search engines in "organic" or "natural" searches (as opposed to paid ads, also known as "sponsored links," which are often found on the right side of search pages or clearly marked as a "sponsored link"). In general, achieving a high rank is based on three criteria: competition, relevancy, and content.

Think of "competition" like popularity. The more popular (talked about, linked to, and clicked on) your offer or website is, the more competitive you are. "Relevancy" is based on how well your offer or site matches the keywords. Your site should include the keyword, or be as close as possible to the keyword, that's being searched. Finally, your "content" should address the question being asked. Your goal is to answer the query as directly as possible. You want the end user to say, "Yes, this is the answer I'm looking for." The sooner you master these three criteria, the higher rank you'll be able to achieve in search results. Mastering the art of search is not impossible; it just takes practice, time, and consistency. Take the time to think about what your potential customers are really asking and how your offer or website answers their questions. Be persistent and consistent, work through the learning curve, and you'll find yourself with a high rank in the search engines.

Search engine marketing (SEM) has grown significantly in the last decade and is a profitable segment of the internet. "With nearly half of every dollar spent on digital advertising going toward search, it remains the most crucial channel for marketers to get right," wrote Forrester Research in its 2018 report on SEM. According to a 2016 study from Search Engine Marketing Professionals Organization, SEM remains the largest digital marketing segment, with social media advertising a close second. Increasingly, ad budgets are being shifted away from offline marketing, such as print, direct mail, and TV advertising, and directed toward online marketing. In 2017, digital ad spending was $209 billion worldwide, the first time it eclipsed TV ad spending (which reached $178 billion in 2017), according to Magna, the research unit of IPG Mediabrands.

There are many search engines out there, and they all differ in structure, search strategy, and efficiency. But according to a January 2018 report by NetMarketShare, 74.5 percent of searches were powered by Google (as we suggested earlier). Another 8 percent were powered by Yahoo! operated Bing.

For the best exposure, be sure your website is listed on both of these sites as well as other players like Ask, Yahoo!, and AOL (yes, it's still around), which command a small amount of search traffic and can be useful if your online business provides a service of some kind that people are likely to search for. To use search engines effectively to draw visitors to your site, the keywords you choose in your domain name, title tag, and the text of your main page can spell the difference in your search engine rankings. Keyword-rich domain names, title tags, and main pages boost traffic. And when using keywords, remember it's important to have them appear naturally. You can check Google AdWords and Google Insights to get a good idea of what sort of words and phrases people search for in your category. Look at Twitter's trending topics for the prior few months for hints as to what people are talking about around the products or services you offer. You can narrow the trending topics menu to regional or even more granular results.

The easiest way to get ranked on search engines is to submit your domain name to various search engines. Maximizing the number of times your URL comes up in a search result is an ongoing process. It takes patience to monitor the search engines by visiting them frequently and studying your log files to see which search engines send you the most traffic. If you need to make changes in your website, particularly your opening page, to move up in the search engine rankings, do so. Spend your time submitting to the most popular and frequented search engines.

Once listed, you can use free online tools, including:

- *SiteReportCard.com*—compares your site with your competition in SEO-friendliness
- *LinkPopularity.com*—lists all sites that have linked back to your domain name in a very basic format
- *iSpionage.com*—shows how you compare to your competitors in terms of search traffic

Keep in mind that Google's share of search is so significant that it's important to spend the most time refining your keywords for Google success—that's the engine where you get the most bang for your buck.

Also keep in mind that the narrower the category, the better your chance of scoring unique visitors; for example, "percussion instruments" and "ice skating dresses" are more specific than "drums" and "sports attire" and have a better chance of scoring clicks. Think about how specific you might get when searching for an item and apply it to your business.

Paid Search Services

Many companies also use paid search services as a supplement to SEM. These services basically allow you to pay to have your website be part of the results of a user's query on a search engine site. There are three types of paid search services: paid submission, pay-for-inclusion, and pay-for-placement.

In paid submission, you can submit your website for review by a search service for a preset fee with the expectation that the site will be accepted and included in that company's search engine—provided it meets the stated guidelines for submission. While paid submissions guarantee a timely review of the submitted site and notice of acceptance or rejection, you're not guaranteed inclusion or a particular placement order in the listings.

Paid inclusion programs allow you to submit your website for guaranteed inclusion in a search engine's database of listings for a set period. While paid inclusion guarantees indexing of submitted pages or sites in a search database, you're not guaranteed that the pages will rank well for particular queries.

In pay-for-placement, you can guarantee a ranking in a search listing for the terms of your choice. Also known as paid placement, paid listings, or sponsored listings, this program guarantees placement in search results. Google also offers pay-per-click search advertisements—and so does Bing. This is one-third of Google's revenue for ads and experts say they pay attention to the success of these ads because of their importance to their own business model.

These programs allow you to bid on the terms you wish to appear for; you then agree to pay a certain amount each time someone clicks on your listing. Costs for pay-for-placement start at around a nickel a click and go up considerably based on how high you want your site to appear—and competition for keywords has the biggest bearing on that. For example, a bid on "web hosting" will result in payment of a few bucks a click if you want to get on the first page of results. But if you're promoting, say, lighthouse tours, you may be able to get on top paying just a dime a click.

In the Google AdWords program, Google sells paid listings that appear above and to the side of its regular results, as well as on its partner sites. Since it may take time for a new site to appear within Google, these advertising opportunities offer a fast way to get listed with the service.

The cost of your Google AdWords campaigns really depends on how much you're willing to pay and how well you know your audience. It all boils down to knowing your own goals and letting Google know what they are. Google will grant the highest position to the advertiser with the highest bid for keywords and the highest clickthrough rate. Minimum costs per click start at just a penny. You can get more insight and tips for getting your ad better positioning at https://support.google.com/adwords/.

The Bing search, known as Bing Ads, doesn't charge you to create an account; you only pay when someone clicks on your ad. The highest position is given to the advertiser with the highest bid for keywords and the highest clickthrough rate. You can budget by the day or the

BUILDING A SOCIAL MEDIA AUDIENCE

By R. L. Adams, *Entrepreneur* contributor and founder of
WanderlustWorker.com

When it comes to marketing anything on social media, without a large following, you won't get very far. Getting there can be hard, but R.L. Adams, an entrepreneur and software engineer, offers these three tips for making the journey to a larger footprint.

1. *Define your niche audience.* Who are you targeting? Get specific. This is important because you'll be curating your content for that intended audience. Everything you do or say needs to geared toward these people. In marketing speak, they call this your demographic. The more you can define your demographic, the higher your chances for success.

2. *Add massive value.* You can't succeed on social media without adding massive amounts of value. There's fierce competition in the marketplace and the stakes are high. Find ways you can share your expertise with others and help the people who follow you. The more you focus on this mentality, the more likely you'll succeed in the long run.

3. *Collaborate.* Find like-minded entrepreneurs on social media who you can collaborate with. Reach out to them. Build a group or find some other way that you can team up with others who might be in a similar situation as yourself or with a similar amount of followers. There is power in numbers. You can't expect to do this yourself or go it alone. Do shout-outs and joint ventures with other people if you want to see sustained growth in followers and fans over time.

campaign, and metrics will help manage your results—with further insight into who turns into a customer once you click. Bing can reach some audiences Google doesn't and claims that 27 percent of its clicks come from searches exclusive to Bing. So, take your time to experiment with both search engines.

Another paid search program to check out is Miva's Merchant program (miva.com), which is a major search player and also offers software and other solutions for small businesses just getting started on the web.

Local Search

Want local customers to find you? Then try local search engine advertising, which lets you target ads to a specific state, city, or even neighborhood. A growing number of small businesses are using local search. In 2017, Forrester Research Inc. found that 71 percent of consumers start their search for a purchase using a search engine, and 74 percent said they use a search engine for "consideration and purchasing" decisions.

Like other search engine advertising, the local variety lets you track your account closely to find out which keywords are most successful at drawing customers and how much you're spending each day.

As you can imagine, the major search engine companies offer local search options, too. You'll find them offered on the main search marketing pages for each site.

MARKETING YOUR SITE

Once you have a plan in place to build confidence in your internet business, get visitors to find your site, streamline customer service issues, and keep your site updated, you can focus on marketing your site more widely beyond the initial web search. Contrary to popular belief, websites don't magically market themselves once they go live. Suppose that you have a website that markets a cookbook that you've created using old family recipes. You've done a good job of keeping your site shallow, and you have a steady flow of buyers. You've done a great job of setting up an efficient website, but you're still limited by the number of customers who actually find and visit it. What's a budding online entrepreneur to do? First, you can start with a little friendly cross-marketing via the use of reciprocal links.

Reciprocal Links

Fortunately, you can actually get other websites to solve this problem for you. One solution is called reciprocal links—and knowing how to use it is absolutely essential for an online business. First, do a search for websites that serve the same customer base that you're interested in. Look for sites that are similar to yours, but also find sites that are related to your topic but not identical. If you're marketing downloadable birthday cards, for example, you should look at sites that are somehow related to birthdays, anniversaries, or any kind of greeting card.

A reciprocal link means that you agree to put a link to another site on your own—and the other site agrees to do the same thing for you. This is different in theory from paid advertising on related sites. This is about relationship building—not paying to play. After all, your goal is to make an income funnel that is easy and cheap to maintain. Spending all your revenue on ads doesn't make sense when you're just starting out. So, if you're selling jewelry, you should want to link with other jewelry sites. But you should also link to sites that aren't exclusively about the product you're selling—for the simple reason that this will expose you to more potential buyers. For example, there are only so many people who go on the internet to buy jewelry. But perhaps more people would buy jewelry if they found out it was available when they visited a local news site or a fashion site or a wedding site.

Your goal is to create a network of sites that are willing to exchange links with you. Always be alert for complementary sites that are willing to exchange links. As you begin your search for appropriate sites, put yourself in the mind of your potential customers and search for the keyword phrases they would use. Once you find some sites that your customers would be likely to visit, start gathering the information you'll need exchange links. For example, you'll need to identify the owners of the site so you can contact them directly. To do that, just go to any domain registry site like www.godaddy.com, a major domain registration site. When you type in the website address you're interested in, you should see the owner's contact information if it has been made public.

Your initial contact can be through an email or social media, but a follow-up phone call is more likely to yield positive results. So try hard to find a contact number on the site you're interested in. Your initial email should be personal, but also very professional. Don't put anything in the subject line that seems like an ad or an offer. Instead, just write "request for further information" or "some questions." In the text of the email itself, mention the owner's name, the name of their business, and the benefits of exchanging links with your site. Keep it crisp and brief. Wait a day or so, and then make a phone call to the recipient of your email.

When you speak to the owner of your prospective link, start by complementing them on their site and use this to introduce your own web business. Explain your site and emphasize how your link will go hand-in-hand with their business. Explain the benefits of exchanging links and respond to any questions they might have. When they agree to exchange reciprocal links, email your HTML code and ask that they do the same.

For your link to be most effective, ask that it be placed on the exit page of the site you're exchanging with. The exit page is the last page that is seen by a majority of visitors to the site. Usually it's the home page, so request that your link be visible at the bottom of the home page if possible. If there's a links page, your contact should be placed there as well. And, of course, you'll want to have a links page on your own site, too.

Creating reciprocal links will also give you more visibility on search engines, because sites are indexed by the number of times they appear as links on other sites. Creating links is probably the number-one thing you should do to bring customers to your site. The fact is, most people return to the same websites 80 percent of the time. They may occasionally surf other sites, but mostly they just look at the sites they've visited before. That means it's difficult to get new people to visit your web page. But if those people go to their favorite site and see a link to your page ready and waiting for them, you're in a much better position to gain them as customers. The more links you have, the more traffic you get, and the more traffic you get, the more passive income you'll receive.

CONSIDER AFFILIATE MARKETING

As far as online passive income streams go, affiliate marketing is one of the fastest and easiest to get started in. Depending on the path you choose, the investment to get up and running can be minimal. It's all dependent on your preferred marketing model and how much you need to outsource as opposed to doing it yourself. And the best part is, you can do this with any kind of site you set up, whether it's a blog, general interest site, or ecommerce store. Once you get your foundation in place, your main ongoing costs are associated with advertising and promoting the products you sell, and you get to choose how much or how little you would like to put into the process.

Affiliate marketing is essentially a way for you to earn cash for promoting and selling items or services without ever having to be responsible for the product, shipping, or fulfillment of the order. You strike a deal with a business, company, or individual to promote their products, and in return, when an item is sold through your affiliate account, you get a commission—a certain percentage or dollar amount for that sale. It's a win-win situation for you and the business: They get free advertising and customers they might not have otherwise reached, and you are compensated for the work you've put in. The commission they pay you is essentially part of their marketing budget. For some companies, it is their exclusive form of marketing.

For the business owner you work with, the pros far outweigh any drawbacks. They decide how much they want to compensate the affiliate, and the cost of the commission is much lower than the costs of traditional advertising. Even the customer comes out a winner in this scenario: Since affiliates and businesses are extremely motivated to sell, sales and coupons are becoming a big part of the affiliate marketing world. It's a low-risk, high-reward setup if you're willing to put in the time and effort. Let's explore how this works.

Personalized Affiliate Links and Cookies

There are two ways an affiliate program will track the prospects you send them:

1. *Personalized affiliate links.* If your affiliate program uses links to track sales, you'll be given a login and a link associated with your account, which you will send to customers so the purchase can be traced back to you.
2. *Cookies.* Some programs use cookies instead of personalized links. Cookies are tiny pieces of data the internet uses to track someone's online habits. It's a way to see where a customer came from and what they bought—think of it like a trail of breadcrumbs showing where customers originated and how they arrived on the site.

Different programs have different duration policies. Some companies will pay you for life any time a prospect you have sent them buys something. Other programs pay only on the initial sale. There are even some programs that have specified time ranges—30, 60, or 90 days—during which they will pay you on purchases made by the prospect you sent them. It is advantageous for you to choose affiliate programs that have cookies that last for at least 30 days so you get credit for all the purchases your leads may make. You should find out this information before you move forward with an affiliate program.

POINTS TO PONDER BEFORE YOU JUMP INTO AFFILIATE MARKETING

As with anything, there are a few drawbacks. If you're not willing to learn and adapt, you will most likely not be a very successful affiliate, but that's true for most things in life. You have to be willing to invest your time, energy, and patience into making it work for you. Small sales here and there are great, but if you want to make this your main source of online passive income, you have to be able to land a lot of sales to make a significant amount of money. You need to think about your efforts as building a business. Two considerations in that vein are creating systems that are set up to get consistent new lead acquisition and choosing higher-margin offers (same amount of work, more money).

For this to be sustainable as a long-term income stream, you need to create promotion strategies that will lead to consistent sales. Just like any business worth getting off the ground, it takes commitment, time, and dedication. This path will be easier for those of you who have some experience with search engine optimization (SEO) or paid traffic generation.

And finally, you really need to choose your affiliates wisely. If the merchant's site is not up to par, slow, buggy, full of errors, and not geared toward making the sale, you will lose out as well. Customers don't have faith or confidence in an online retailer that can't properly run its website. This issue is out of your hands, which is why it's important to take it into account before becoming an affiliate. Take a look around the site and ask yourself, "Would I feel comfortable buying from here?" If the answer is no, you may want to reconsider becoming an affiliate for that business. When you're an affiliate, you are at the mercy of the merchant/business that is selling the actual product.

TYPES OF AFFILIATE OFFERS

In reality, any business can create an affiliate program and recruit affiliates as part of their marketing strategy. However, most offers you will be exposed to can be lumped into three categories: products, services, and stores. We'll briefly explore the differences that will help you identify which options might be the best fit for you.

Products

There are two types of online products you can be an affiliate for: physical and digital. The marketing strategies you will employ won't really change either way, but they do each come with their own sets of pros and cons.

Physical Products

Pros: Not all consumers buy digital products, but pretty much all consumers buy physical products. If you choose a product that is in demand, made by a trusted brand, and sold through a credible online store, the selling is really already done for you.

Cons: The biggest cons to physical products are the shipping cost and the fact that it takes some time for the product to arrive. Also, there are certain products that consumers want to be able to touch and experience before they buy. That can sometimes hamper an online purchase.

Digital Products

Pros: One of the biggest advantages of a digital product is instant gratification. The consumer can immediately dig in and enjoy the product they purchased while they are excited about it. If you are in tune with your prospects' problems and have a digital product that gives them the solution to that problem, conversions can be really high. No shipping costs are another plus.

Cons: Digital products are often swimming among a lot of competition that you need to stand out from. Also, you're at the mercy of the retailer when it comes to making sure the product downloads properly. Sometimes digital products are so complicated they overwhelm the consumer, which can hinder additional sales from that prospect.

Services

When most people think of affiliate marketing, the first thing that usually comes to mind is selling products. However, there are also many services people pay for online that have affiliate programs. Some examples are:

- ❦ Financial services like tax preparation
- ❦ Social media and digital marketing services

- Professional services (hosting, payment processing, etc.)
- Travel-related services like Hotels.com and Travelocity

Storewide Programs

There are tons of stores that will give you commissions on the entire purchase made by a consumer you send to their site. This is great because it gives you the flexibility to market just one product they sell and still get credit for anything else your prospect adds to their cart, or you can just promote the entire store in general.

WHERE TO FIND AFFILIATE PRODUCTS AND SERVICES TO PROMOTE

When you're first getting started, try your hand at some of the proven affiliate marketing networks before tackling the smaller markets. They are all fairly similar in intent, but each one has its own processes, requirements, and restrictions. It's very important that you take the time to read through how their program works to make sure it's the best choice for you.

Some aspects to research include:

- *Sign-up criteria.* Each network or program will have its own sign-up criteria for you to be accepted as an affiliate. You may not initially qualify for some, but keep trying, as others will take you straight off.
- *Payment arrangements.* The payment policies for each program can differ. You might get instant, seven-day, two-week, or monthly payments, and in some cases these won't start until 60 days have passed. Understand your terms so you won't be left holding the bag for advertising costs you've incurred.
- *Restrictions.* Make sure you understand the rules and restrictions and that they will fit into your passive online business model.

If you have any questions or concerns, the time to ask them is before you sign up, because after that you're bound to the terms and services you agreed to.

Some Popular Programs

There are a lot of programs out there for you to research, explore, and experiment with. It is vitally important for you to take some time to research these sites and figure out which one will be best for you. We could give you a list of pros and cons for each one, but your situation is unique, so only you can decide which resource makes the most sense. Here are a few that are popular:

- DealGuardian (http://dealguardian.com)
- JVZoo (www.jvzoo.com)
- ClickBank (www.clickbank.com)
- CJ Affiliate (www.cj.com)
- ShareASale (www.shareasale.com)
- PeerFly (https://peerfly.com)
- Amazon Associates (https://affiliate-program.amazon.com)

The great thing about people who play in this space is that they are very vocal about what they like and don't like. You can do a search for each of these programs and find a lot of aspects that people love and dislike about each one. If you take the time to do a little research, you should be able to identify which one will be the right fit for you and the direction you want to take your business.

HOW TO EVALUATE WHICH AFFILIATE PROGRAMS ARE RIGHT FOR YOU

Which programs are best for you has a lot to do with the type of industry you are marketing in. Who is your target market? You want to pick programs and offers that make sense for your market. The very first thing you want to think about is whether the offer fits the needs of your target market. Outside that, it's really about choosing a program that has processes and guidelines you feel in alignment with. There isn't a magic pill to give you regarding selection. Now that you know the important criteria, you just need to be sure to do your due diligence.

There are lots of affiliate marketing programs out there and more are coming online every day, but as mentioned above, not all are created equal. There's no way to go through all of them and tell you which are legitimate and which are a scam, but here are a few things you should look for.

If an affiliate program is asking you for money upfront, it is a scam. Never hand over money to become an affiliate; it's a mutually beneficial arrangement, and no one should be paying for it.

If the site is filled with pop-up ads and banner advertisements, it's best to steer clear. Legitimate affiliate marketing programs do not need to market themselves so heavily.

If an affiliate program begs you to bring other affiliates into the mix, that's not affiliate marketing, it's multilevel marketing (MLM), which is a completely different beast (you'll read about it in Chapter 10).

HOW TO CHOOSE AN AFFILIATE OFFER

Choosing the right offer is critical to your success. Here are some tips from successful affiliate marketers:

- *Product and service quality.* Choose offers you would be proud to have your name behind. You want your prospects to consider you a credible source to return to for suggestions of things to buy.
- *The merchant website.* Don't trust the statistics the merchant's website claims at face value. Take a look around the website and observe what your experience would be if you were visiting as a first-time buyer. Is it laid out well? Are you able to find what you're looking for? Are you having a good experience? Would you return?
- *Commissions.* It goes without saying, but the better the commissions, the more enticing the offer. This could be in margins or longer cookie durations.
- *EPC.* This stands for "earnings per click" and represents how much on average the affiliates make from the sale. Make a point to choose a site that offers you a high EPC.
- *Return percentage.* Choose offers that have low return percentages.
- *Deep linking.* Sites that don't allow deep linking hinder an affiliate's conversions. You want to promote offers that allow you to

link directly to the offer landing page so you get more conversions.

- ⊛⟶ *Create marketing content.* Don't just rely on the content the merchant provides. Create high-quality content your competitors can't compete with.
- ⊛⟶ *Traffic variations.* Don't rely on only one traffic source.

PROMOTING YOUR AFFILIATE OFFERS

Your job is to drive interested traffic to these offers, and the more you do that, the more money everyone makes. There are many, many ways to go about that. So, while marketing skills are essential, they can be learned. You don't even need to have a website. Many people successfully sell affiliate offers through social media platforms. It just depends on what your chosen business model is.

There are numerous ways you can effectively market affiliate products, but here we're going to talk about the most common and accessible methods for those just getting started. As you gain more skills in promoting products on the internet, you'll be able to scale your efforts and create larger paydays. Let's look at several methods successful affiliates use to promote their offers.

Blogging

If you have a blog or want to go this route, it's important to understand that in order for this method to work, you'll have to be consistent when it comes to posting and building your audience. Simply showing up once a week to post some random affiliate links won't yield many results. You won't be a trusted voice recommending anything. On the other hand, if you build an engaged, interested blog community that is used to receiving quality content and the occasional offer from you, you will do well.

If you're managing a blog and building a list in a specific market, you have the flexibility to mix up the type of content you are posting. It's great to write content about your offers, but you can also actually place the affiliate ads right on the page of your blog. You can even add navigation that groups different offers by topics and categories. This is especially useful for those of you who want to build out an authority site in your chosen industry.

Email Marketing

Affiliate marketing via email is one of the oldest and most effective methods to make money, assuming you have a relevant email list you can market to. Having a list of several thousand trusted followers can be akin to having an affiliate annuity: email and make money. That said, you have to constantly grow and nurture that list and regularly deliver value that is not an affiliate offer. Do that, and you'll succeed. If you employ a "churn and burn" email marketing campaign, you'll eventually lose your list and your income, and you could get blacklisted in Google so that all your emails get filtered into the spam section of your prospects' email accounts.

If you don't have a list yet, it's definitely worth the time and effort to build one. The ability to send out one email to multiple people promoting the product(s) you are interested in selling is an easy and effective way to make good money for little effort. Experts in the field estimate you could expect at least $1 per month from each subscriber on a well-put-together list of clients. What other type of marketing tool can provide that? Not many.

Many people buy email lists. This is not advisable when you're starting. Buying email lists can be really great or really terrible. It takes some experience to get a handle on quality resources you can trust vs. ones you should avoid.

Paid Advertising

Digital marketer Ryan Deiss often says: "If you want traffic, you go to the traffic store and you buy it." Paid traffic is really efficient, but it's also overwhelming when you are starting, and mistakes can be costly. Find outsourced solutions you trust, put some time and money into taking a course, or learn the ins and outs of any of the paid traffic platforms you might want to use. The good news is that most of them have their own tutorials and training videos because they want you to use them. They make money whether you do or not! Some of our favorite paid traffic platforms are:

- Google AdWords (www.google.com/adwords)
- Google Display Network (www.google.com/ads/displaynetwork)
- Facebook Ads (www.facebook.com/business/products/ads)
- LinkedIn Ads (www.linkedin.com/ads)
- Twitter Ads (https://biz.twitter.com/ad-products)
- Pinterest Promoted Pins (https://business.pinterest.com/en/promote-on-pinterest)
- Banner ads on relevant websites (which you find thanks to the link-building tips you learned in the last chapter)

Free Advertising

Paid ads are not your only option. However, keep in mind that the old adage "You get what you pay for" often rings true when it comes to paid vs. free ads online. Here are a few ways you can score free advertising, some of which are easy to implement, others of which might require more effort than you're willing to spend if you're shooting for the ultimate passive experience:

- *Free ads.* Ads on free sites like Craigslist (www.craigslist.org/about/sites) and US Free Ads (www.usfreeads.ws), among many others, are indeed free but require a constant investment of time, therefore, they are not recommended as your primary advertising avenue.
- *Video marketing.* Many affiliates who have some video skills are making healthy incomes creating short promotional videos, uploading them to YouTube, then promoting the video. This can work well if you are skilled at getting your videos to rank highly in YouTube's results.
- *YouTube partner program.* This is connected to your Google AdSense account. The basic premise is that YouTube shares the

ad revenue they collect from viewers who see the ads that have been placed on your video.

&~ *Social media marketing.* Marketing your affiliate links on social media networks through organic engagement, as opposed to paid advertising platforms, is a great way to build a list and make sales. The most important thing to remember is that if you build a list on a social media platform, you need to also make a plan to monetize that list. Often when people are starting they create a great following but don't understand how to monetize it.

Social media audiences are very attuned to when they are being marketed to, so seller beware. Strive to regularly engage your followers with interesting information that isn't selling anything. A side note: If you are a member of large Facebook groups that are related to the topic of your offer, you might be able to post a link if you have been a valuable contributor to the group. You can even offer to share commissions with the group owner. On front-runners like Facebook, the key is to be aboveboard and as transparent as possible and carefully adhere to their rules to stay compliant.

Which platform makes the most sense for you has a lot to do with the market you're in. You'll want to do some research and find out where your target buyers hang out and which communication channels they use most.

HOW MUCH MONEY CAN I MAKE?

It shouldn't surprise you that, just like most other business models, the amount of money you can and will make is variable. Some days, weeks, and months will be better than others; you'll need a long-term average to really gauge how much you're making. Holidays are usually a big time for sales, and summer is usually when a slump occurs (unless you're selling swim gear). As with anything, what you put in is what you get out. It's a way to make passive income online, not a get-rich-quick scheme, but if you stick with it and make the right choices, you could bring in a significant amount of money in no time.

Your odds of success will be much higher if you are really in tune with the intention, also known as the "why to buy," of the buyers in your chosen market. Whether you already have some experience with marketing and driving traffic or whether you'll be learning it for the first time, keep your eye on their intention. Why are customers seeking what you're selling? What do the demographics of your buying audience tell you? What is their ultimate need? Understanding this kind of intention will help you not just get in front of your target buyers, but also get in front of them with messaging that speaks to the heart of what they are looking for.

In the end, affiliate marketing is not particularly difficult, but it's also not an easy, quick, or even painless process. If it were, everybody would be doing it. If you're looking for a fast, get-rich-quick scheme, this probably isn't it. But if you're willing to put in the effort, time, and dedication, the benefits can be substantial for you, your brand, and your financial future.

PARTING THOUGHTS

Building and hosting a passively profitable website is just one key to opening the door to a sustained passive income model. As your site evolves and you tweak it to maximize its earning potential, you will eventually hit a sweet spot where the site is generating money with minimal effort from you. It may involve a good deal of legwork at the beginning, but eventually, a profitable website will run on its own with little maintenance. A good website business is definitely one of the best ways to generate revenue, but it's far from your only profit-making opportunity. In the next chapter, you'll learn why the stock market has always been one of the most appealing and hands-on business investments. More important, you'll find out how you can immediately start building passive income from real estate, even with no experience and very little capital.

CHAPTER FIVE

MAKING YOUR MARK IN THE STOCK MARKET

So far in our discussion of creating passive income on the internet, you've read about investing in yourself. You've seen how a relatively small investment in a website business can have a consistent payoff. Later, you'll read more about the concept of self-investment, but in the next four chapters, we'll be looking at passive income from some other very important sources, starting here with stock investments, then later with real estate.

Both kinds of investing (stocks and real estate) are proven vehicles for successful investments, and especially for the creation of passive income. By putting some time, some thought, and a comparatively small amount of money into them, you can definitely bring greater financial freedom into your life. But it won't happen by itself. Knowledge and discipline are essential—and those are two elements we're going to focus on in the next chapters. But before you start jumping into day trading or interviewing potential investment brokers, you should consider how stock investing is different from investing in real estate.

Stocks and real estate have some basic similarities, but they're also very different kinds of investments. For example, suppose you get a mortgage on a piece of rental property. Your actual ownership of the property may be very small, depending on the amount of your down payment. If the cost of the property is $100,000 and you put $10,000 down, you own 10 percent of the property. The rest belongs to the lender. When rent is paid by the tenant, you can use that income in a number of different ways. You can spend it, save it, or reinvest it to pay down your mortgage and own a larger piece of the property. In some ways, the stock market is very similar. When you purchase shares in a company, you now own a small percentage of that firm. If the shares pay dividends, you can spend, save, or reinvest the income—just as you can in real estate. Those are the similarities between stocks and real estate; and now, here are two important differences. First, real estate is *real* in a way that stocks are not. A house is something that you can see with your eyes and touch with your hands. It is a tangible product. But stock ownership is much more symbolic. As tangible evidence of your investment, you get nothing more than a certificate—and usually not even that. Most likely, a receipt from your broker will be the only evidence of your purchase. Of course, both a real estate deal and a stock purchase are legal and binding business transactions, but the symbolic nature of stocks has some important psychological effects.

An even more important difference between stocks and real estate involves the liquidity of the two investments. Simply put, it's a lot easier and faster to sell your stocks than it is to sell your house—and for many people, it's also a lot more exciting. And that's what you will learn about in this chapter—how to make that excitement put money in your pocket. But even exciting methods of making passive income need a plan.

HAVE A PLAN

This leads us to the first key principle of stock market investing: You need to have a plan, and you need to stick with it. Before you make your first stock purchase, you must know what your goals are and not lose sight of those goals. Remember, your goal is to create passive income so that you can achieve financial freedom. Your goal is not to make a quick buck or to make lots of exciting stock trades every day. The fact is, you could have the best trading strategy in the world, but if you don't stick to your game plan, it will be worthless.

Going back to what you read in Chapter 1, you know that before you start anything, you need to understand what motivates you and what your goals are. Do you want to invest money in a mutual index fund or low-yield-but-safe portfolio, then set it aside and forget about it? Or are you more of a risk taker who wants to actively participate in the trading of stocks on a regular basis? Do you want to self-manage or hire someone to do the legwork for you? Depending on your answers to these questions, you can choose to go with a low-risk, long-term strategy. Or perhaps you have a longer lead time and choose to invest in an index fund geared toward higher risk early that levels off to a medium- to low-risk mix over time. The possibilities for strategy are endless here and greatly dependent on your goals.

Once you have your strategy clearly in mind, you need to think of it as a machine that runs all by itself for a stipulated period of time. You can watch it very closely, but you can't interfere with its operation. Does that sound like a difficult thing to do? The answer might not be as easy as you think. To see why, consider the following example.

Imagine you had created a software program for betting on horse races online. You tested this program against the results of hundreds of horse races going back many years, and you know that over the long run it will generate a positive return. But the program only bets on a select number of races, and it also only bets on the favorite in each race. So the return is relatively small—between 10 and 15 percent. Of course, a consistent return of any amount is very unusual in horse racing, where almost everyone loses money. And 10 to 15 percent is also quite good compared to what you would get from a bank. So you should be happy, right? Not many people can say that they've beaten the races.

But suppose a few days go by and you notice that the machine is not making a profit. At first, you're not worried—but as the losing streak continues, you start to get a little worried. What if you made a mistake in the program? Or what if the research you did on past performances wasn't as accurate as you thought? To make matters worse, suppose that while your bets on the favorites were losing, all the long shots were coming in. You've been risking your money in the hope of making 10 percent, and now other people are winning at 10-to-1 or even 30-to-1. Under those conditions, do you think you might be tempted to deviate from your game plan? Do you think your fear of loss might overcome your confidence in success?

Now let's look at another possibility. Suppose your betting program performs exactly as you expected. Week after week, it's generating a 10 or 15 percent profit. You don't feel fear in this situation, but you might start to feel a bit of greed. You might start wondering how much more money you could be making if you started placing some side bets on long shots. True, you had planned to be very conservative with your passive income returns—but now you start thinking about all the money you can make if you take just a few chances. And then, when those chances don't pay off, you decide to take some even bigger chances in order to recover your losses.

I think you can see where this leads. Fear, greed, or the desire for action cause investors to abandon what could have been successful strategies. Far too often, experienced investors get so caught up in the day-to-day performance of their portfolio that they lose sight of the big picture of making long-term profits. The desire for constant action is probably responsible for more stock market losses than any other factor, especially since trades can now be made literally in a matter of seconds.

If you have a solid investing plan, you need to go on automatic pilot. Pull away from the emotional urge to win on a day-to-day basis and look at the big picture. Of course, this assumes you have a solid plan—and that's no small assumption. If you're at a total loss for a plan and you don't have endless startup capital, check out some of the ideas below that you can start today for a grand or less.

GOT A GRAND? TRY THESE INVESTMENTS

If you're sitting on at least $1,000 and it's scratching an itch in your pocket, consider investing it rather than spending it on something frivolous. But the question that then beckons is: Can you really make money investing with just a $1,000? And can you do it quickly?

The answer to that is a resounding yes.

While there are plenty of ways you can make money fast, actually making money by investing with just $1,000 might present more challenges, and frankly, more risks. That is, of course, unless you know what you're doing.

However, all risks aside, even if you're living paycheck to paycheck while dealing with fatigue and exhaustion because you're trading your time for money, you can still likely conjure up $1,000 to put toward an investment that you can eventually turn into a passive income stream.

Yet before you dive in, there are some mindset principles you need to adhere to. Moving beyond the scarcity mentality is crucial. Too many of us live our lives with the notion that there's never enough of things to go around. We don't have enough time, money, connections, or opportunities to grow and live life at a higher level.

That's just a belief system. Think and you shall become. If you think you can't get rich or even make a sizable amount of money by investing it into lucrative short-term investment vehicles, then it's much more of a mindset issue than anything else. You don't need to invest a lot of money with any of the following strategies.

Sure, having more money to invest would be ideal. But it's not necessary. As long as you can identify the right strategy that works for you, all you need to do is scale. What does that mean? It's similar to building an offer online, identifying the right conversion rate through optimization, then scaling that out. If you know you can invest a dollar and make two dollars, you'll continue to invest a dollar. In other words, you scale up your investment strategy when you implement a long-term plan that can be replicated and built upon.

Start small. Try different methods, different strategies. Track and analyze your results. Don't get so caught up on how you're going to get wildly rich overnight. That won't happen. But if you can leverage one of the following methods to make money by investing small, short bursts of capital, then all you have to do is scale. Plain and simple. You don't have to overthink it. If you have a $1,000 to invest, you can make money a variety of ways. But there are some methods that trump others. The play here is speed. We're not talking about long-term buy-hold strategies. Those are terrific if you're looking to invest your capital over at least a two- to five-year period. We're talking about ways you can make money fast so you can build your investment bucket to continue investing for later passive, long-term gains.

Even when it comes to markets that might take time to move or have longer cycles, investments can often turn into realized profits and quick gains by leveraging the right strategies. What's the right strategy?

Raghee Horner, futures and currency expert at Simpler Trading, says that "long-term interest rates are the next big trade," while Jim Cramer, host of CNBC's investment show *Mad Money,* says "there are tons of people who are late to trends by nature and adopt a trend after it's no longer in fashion." By jumping in and out of long-term investments like that, you're far more likely to lose your shirt than if you time your short-term plays just right.

It's not so much about trying to catch the latest trend. Investing your money is more about paying careful attention to indicators that can really move the needle in the short term as opposed to the longer term. It's also about leveraging and hedging your investments the right way without putting too much risk on the line. The following investment strategies might help you do just that.

Play the Stock Market

Day trading (buying and selling stocks on the same day, often in online transactions) is not for the faint of heart. It takes grit and determination. It takes understanding the different market forces at play. This isn't something intended for amateurs. But if learned and learned well, it is a way you can quickly—within the span of hours—make a significant amount of money with a relatively small investment.

There are also ways to hedge your bets when it comes to playing the stock market. Whether you play the general market or trade penny stocks (stocks valued under $5 per share), ensure that you set stop-loss limits to cut any potential for significant depreciations. A *stop-loss limit* is simply an order you set with your broker to sell stock when it hits a specific price. Now if you're an advanced trader, you likely understand that market makers often move stocks to play into either our fear of failure or our greed. And they'll often push a stock down to a certain price to enhance that fear and play right into their pockets.

When it comes to penny stocks, this is further exaggerated. So you have to understand what you're doing and be able to analyze the market forces and make significant gains. Pay attention to moving averages. Often, when stocks break through 200-day moving averages (the average price of a security over a certain period of time), there's potential for either a large upside or a big downside.

Trade Commodities

You can also participate in the trading of commodities, ranging from agricultural products like wheat, corn, coffee, cocoa, and sugar to hard commodities like gold and silver. Trading commodities like gold and silver present a rare opportunity, especially when they're trading at the lower end of their five-year range. Metrics like that give a strong indication on where commodities might be heading. Not always, but usually. Carolyn Boroden of trading how-to site Fibonacci Queen says,

"I have long-term support and timing in the silver markets," because silver is a solid hedge on inflation. Plus, commodities like silver are tangible assets that people can hold onto." In other words, a hard commodity such as silver or gold tends to hold value, even during a rough economic patch. Keep in mind, however, that commodity trading can be risky, depending on your level of knowledge in the futures market and outside factors like the weather.

The fundamentals of economics drive the price of commodities. As supply dips, demand increases and prices rise. Any disruption to a supply chain has a severe impact on prices. For example, a health scare to livestock can significantly alter prices as scarcity reins free. However, livestock and meat are just one form of commodities.

Other commodities include things like metals, energy, and agriculture. To invest, you can use an exchange like the London Metal Exchange, the Chicago Mercantile Exchange, and many others. Often, investing in commodities means investing in futures contracts. Effectively, that's a prearranged agreement to buy a specific quantity at a specific price in the future. These are leveraged contracts, providing both a big upside and a potential for a large downside. So be extra careful.

Trade Cryptocurrencies

Cryptocurrencies, digital assets you can use like money online (think bitcoin, for example), are on the rise. While trading them might seem risky due to industry concerns about potential fraud and security issues, as well as lack of protection if your investment goes bust, you could limit some fallout from a poorly timed trade if you hedge your bets here. There are plenty of platforms for trading cryptocurrencies, but before you dive in, educate yourself. Find courses on platforms like Udemy, Kajabi, or Teachable, and learn the intricacies of trading cryptocurrencies like bitcoin, ethereum, litecoin, and others.

While there are over 3,000 cryptocurrencies in existence, only a handful really matter. Find an exchange, research the trading patterns, look for breakouts of long-term moving averages, and get busy trading.

You can use exchanges like Coinbase, Kraken, and CEX.io, along with many others, to make the actual trades.

Which cryptocurrency should you be trading at the end of the day? Ethereum and litecoin. While all the buzz is about bitcoin, these two cryptocurrencies are established and are holding steady, without the frenzy. Will the frenzy hit them next? Possibly. But the only way to find out is to get in on the so-called ground floor.

Use Peer-to-Peer Lending

Peer-to-peer lending (borrowing and lending money without the use of a financial institution) is a hot investment vehicle these days. While you might not get rich investing in a peer-to-peer lending network, you could definitely make a bit of coin. Which lending platform do you use? Today, there are loads. But the most popular ones include LendingClub, Peerform, and Prosper.

How does this work? Peer-to-peer lending platforms allow you to give small bursts of capital to businesses or individuals, while collecting an interest rate on the return. You get more money than if you had placed it in a savings account, plus your risk is limited because the proprietary algorithms on each platform evaluate the potential investments for you.

Once you identify a potential investment opportunity, you can dig in and do some research about the company before deciding whether to invest. And on most platforms, you can either take the deal or not. You'll be able to make the decision to invest based on a variety of well-thought-out data, including a risk assessment, which includes the borrower's employment and credit history.

Trade Options

You can also trade options, which are designed to give the buyer the option (but not obligation) to buy or sell a stock asset at a specific time and on a specific date. When it comes to options, Tom Sosnoff, co-founder of options brokerage TastyTrade, says, "trade small and trade often." What type should you trade? There are loads of vehicles like Forex and stocks. When it comes to options, the best way to make money by investing is to jump in at around 15 days before corporate earnings are released. What type should you buy?

The optimal time to sell money calls is the day before the company releases its earnings. There's just so much excitement and anticipation around earnings that it typically drives up the price, giving you a consistent winner. But don't hold through the earnings. That's a crapshoot and a gamble you don't want to take if you're not a seasoned investor, says John Carter from trading megasite Simpler Trading.

In the next section, we'll look at the different types of investors who can create passive income from stocks. You'll find out why some investor strategies work and others don't. There's a good chance this will help you make some money, and there's an even better chance that it will keep you from losing a lot more. Just as you need to know your "why," you also need to know what kind of investor you are at heart.

KNOW YOUR "WHY"

Everyone thinks they have the magic strategy for making money in the stock market. But the truth is, what works for one person may not apply to another. So before we jump into talking about strategies, you should first remember one guiding principle. The golden rule of stock market investing is very simple: Know why you're in the market in the first place, and know why you're making any individual trade. Since you know that your purpose is to create passive income, you can concentrate on the second part of the golden rule. Since many investors are not sure why they bought a stock in the first place, if the price suddenly falls they're not sure what to do next. On the other hand, if an investor knows why he or she made the purchase, the decision to sell, hold, or even buy more won't be based on day-to-day price fluctuations. Suppose, for example, that you bought ten shares of Microsoft. If your buy was based on a justifiable expectation that the price was about to go up in the short term, you might want to sell if the price goes down instead. You might conclude that what you expected was based on wrong information. But if you bought Microsoft because you believed it was an undervalued stock, and if the conditions have not changed, you might actually want to buy more—because now the stock is even more undervalued. If you remember nothing else, remember your "why." It's your North star and should guide your buying and selling decisions. Then you can move on to figuring out what type of investor you are.

WHAT'S YOUR INVESTOR PROFILE?

Let's look at a few investor types and the plusses and minuses of each—warts and all. You'll see very quickly why some are better than others. But once again, don't be too quick to pass judgment. It's easy to fall into stock investment traps, and it's not always easy to see the solid opportunities.

The Brother-in-Law Investor

We'll begin with a common investor profile that's sometimes called "the brother-in-law" investor. Joe's story below is a prime example:

> Last Saturday my brother-in-law called me with a tip on a great stock. He heard about it from his neighbor, then he checked out the company on the internet. It sounded like a chance to make some money, but I would really have to act fast. The stock was going to start going up as soon as trading started on Monday, so every minute I waited was potentially going to cost me money. Fortunately, I was able to immediately open an online trading account so I could get in as quickly as possible. Will the stock pay good dividends? I'm not sure since I didn't get the chance to really research it, so I'll just have to go with the advice I was given.

As you can see, there are obvious dangers in following the brother-in-law strategy: pressure to act quickly and lack of information can easily lead to poor decisions or, at the very least, hasty ones that may not bear out the market. But the biggest red flag to notice here is how the internet is brought in to validate what might otherwise be an obviously foolish course to follow. In fact, today the internet can actually take the place of the brother-in-law, or the neighbor, or the conversation you overheard in a restaurant. For some reason, what people read online can cause them to instantly take action, even if it's something they would never do otherwise. Never let the internet—or your brother-in-law—be the deciding factor in a stock market decision. Try to get as much information as possible from a variety of sources, not just over the backyard fence. Then follow the stock for a period of time. See how it reacts to changing financial news. Pay special attention to the volume of trading for your stock. After all, if no one is buying it, the price can't go up. If you're still interested in the stock after several weeks, and you're sure it fits into your strategy of creating passive income, then you're ready to make a confident purchase. Remember the old adage: Trust but verify.

The Value Investor

People who buy stocks based on information about a specific company, independent of the market as a whole, are called "value investors" or "fundamental investors." Margaret is such an investor:

> *When I decide to invest in a company's stock, I base my decision on facts about that specific company. I'm investing in the inherent value of the business, as expressed by its proven ability to make money right now—not at some point in the future, but in its most recent annual report. Most people define value investing as the process of searching for stocks with a low ratio of price-to-book value, or a low price-to-earnings ratio. In contrast, stocks with a high price-to-book value or a high price-to-earnings ratio are growth stocks—or if they're not growth stocks, they could also be called just plain bad investments.*

While doing basic research is always a good idea for any investor, the value investor really digs in deeply to find out about the company or companies they are putting their money in. For example, you may be concerned with environmental issues and want to make sure you only invest in funds or individual stocks of companies that are eco-friendly. Perhaps you want to ensure that none of your money will be going to a fund that doesn't represent your personal ideals and beliefs.

Then you will most likely be a value investor, as you'll do the proper due diligence before signing away your investment funds.

The Technical Investor

The opposite of the value investor is the so-called technical investor. This is someone who pays less attention to the fundamentals of a specific stock than to the up or down trends of the entire market at that moment. Technical investors were once called chartists, because their main activity was making and studying charts of stock prices. Today, all this information is online. Many different programs are used to reveal patterns in the past performance of the market. The hope is that those patterns will carry over into the future. Mark is an example of a technical investor:

> When I purchase or trade a stock, my first strategy is to spend time tracking how it performs both as a part of various index funds and as an individual stock. I like to see how it reacts to market changes before I commit. For example, I might go back even a few years to check the performance of a stock on days that major historical events occurred, like elections, hurricanes, or sales/closings of major corporations. That way, I get a picture of how that stock might react in similar market conditions.

It would be fair to say that the three kinds of people we've just discussed—the so-called brother-in-law investor, the value investor, and the technical investor—comprise the majority of individual stockholders. But there are also many variations of these three categories. For example, there are technical investors who study trends of the Dow Jones Industrial Average, and there are others who chart the interest rates set by the Federal Reserve. There are fundamental investors who buy stocks when a company's earnings have reached a new high—while others will sell for the same reason, figuring there's nowhere to go except down. And an increasing number of investors combine the different methods into their own personal style.

Whatever approach you take, the most important thing is knowing why you bought a particular stock. If you bought it on the recommendation of your neighbor, be happy about it and recognize that this is why you made the purchase. It's a good idea to actually write down your reasons for making a buy. Tell the reason to your spouse. Tape it on your bathroom mirror. Keep a journal. But whatever the reason, don't kid yourself. Have a strategy, stick with it, and accept responsibility for whatever it brings.

THE MUTUAL INVESTOR: SAFETY IN NUMBERS

If relying on a few individual single investments isn't your thing, you can always buy into a mutual fund. So far, you've been reading about the single-investor approach (with the variations we mentioned above). We've been talking about individual investors—that is, people who decide for themselves which stocks they're going to buy or sell. In a very real sense, the strategies used by individual investors are less important than the fact that they are indeed individuals. Why is this so important? It's because the real heavy hitters in the stock market are not individuals but pension funds, banks insurance companies, and other billion-dollar institutional investors. Sometimes these institutional investors are called elephants, and that's only partly because they're big. Think of a swimming pool. If an elephant steps into the pool, the water level is going to rise. Well, the same thing is going to happen when an elephant-size institutional investor makes a huge stock purchase. The price will go up. By the same token, if the elephant gets out of the swimming pool, the water level goes down just like the price of a stock goes down when a big mutual fund unloads it. Compared to the elephants' influence on stock prices, the effect of an individual investor is more like that of a mouse or even a gnat.

So what does this mean for you as an individual investor? To answer this, we need to look back at a point we made at the start of this chapter. We spoke about the differences between investing in stocks and real estate, and the fact that stocks are a much more liquid investment tool. If you want to buy or sell a stock, you can do it in less than an hour. If you want to buy or sell a house, you may need a year or more. Because of the huge effect that institutional investors have on the stock market, there's a strong argument for simply buying shares of a big mutual fund. Because if you can't beat them, why not join them?

To bring a stream of passive income into your life, a good mutual fund is a great way to start. The administrators of the fund will do all the work for you. They will make all the decisions about when to buy and when to sell. All you have to do is collect the quarterly dividends. It sounds very simple, and it actually is. There are only a few small complications. First, buying a mutual fund does not entirely eliminate you from the decision-making process. You still have to decide which mutual fund to buy, and since funds can do better or worse just like individual companies, there's no guarantee you'll get the results you hoped for. With many funds, there is also a minimum investment required, and sometimes there is a penalty for withdrawing money before a certain amount of time has passed. To some extent, both of these requirements run counter to what may have originally attracted you to the stock market. You may have liked the fact that you could get into the market for $50 or $100, but now the fund tells you that you have to invest thousands. You may also have appreciated the fact that you could quickly cash in your investment at any time, but now the fund may charge you for doing so.

The seemingly intelligent choice of investing in a mutual fund may come with some frustrations. But if you're the type of person who wants to invest in the stock market in the first place, there's one more big problem with mutual funds. Simply put, they're boring. Months and years can go buy with very little change of any kind. True, a major goal of our program is to free you from spending all your time at work. But many stock market investors crave action. Never making trades can seem like more work than making them. However, if you truly want a "plug and play" experience with little day-to-day maintenance (or none at all, if you use the services of a broker), then throwing your money in the mutual fund bucket is the way to go.

And that's exactly what you should expect from going the mutual fund route—ease of use and a relatively low-maintenance experience. Next, let's talk about what else you should really expect from your stock market investments. What you should expect, by the way, may be something different from what you might hope for—and it's certainly different from what you might dream about. The good news is, it's also very different from what you might fear.

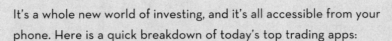

TRADING APPS FOR EASY INVESTING

It's a whole new world of investing, and it's all accessible from your phone. Here is a quick breakdown of today's top trading apps:

- *Seedrs*. An equity crowdfunding platform that is meant to make investing easy. It is a platform for startup owners and potential backers. Investing in startups is risky, but immensely rewarding. Seedrs simplifies its process by providing the means and tools to make informed decisions and crowdfund safely. Upon signup, all you need to do is follow your favorite startup's campaign and press a few buttons to invest. Amounts start from as little as $10.

- *Acorns*. Speaking of Wall Street, Acorns is a unique way to invest in stocks and bonds on a micro level. Acorns combines saving and investing by automatically investing your spare change from every purchase you make throughout your day. For example, if you spend $4.60 on lunch, it rounds the amount to $5 and invests the additional 40 cents. So, instead of stacking large sums, you plant small seeds in Acorns' investment program.

- *Stash*. Seeking to empower a new generation of investors, Stash allows you to invest your money in the industries you support. You start with as little as $5, and you have total control over where your money goes. Stash offers over 30 baskets of investment, so you can choose if you want to support environmentally friendly companies or someone from the entertainment, travel, and leisure industries. Stash is

TRADING APPS, CONTINUED

the ultimate novice investor's tool because it also provides tips and tools on how to build a sound personal portfolio. Pricing starts at just $1 per month, including a free trial month. Portfolios over $5,000 pay a 0.25 percent annual fee.

↞ *M1 Finance.* This app is a long-term automated investment program (also known as a robo-advisor) for people who want their money to work for them. In brief, it incorporates control and customization with the automation and cost structure of typical robo-advisors. The M1 process goes like this: You open a free account and choose a portfolio template that fits your goals. For example, you can select a plan for retirement or for income earners, which replicates the security-holding movements of American depository banks. If you do not like any option, you can create your own investment pie. The initial investment is at least $100. The first $1,000 is handled free of charge. Investments up to $100,000 incur a 0.25 percent annual fee and accounts over $100,000 pay a 0.15 percent annual fee.

↞ *Robinhood.* Offering the ability to buy and sell stocks for free, this app seeks to disrupt traditional stock brokers. How does the app make money then? For $6 per month, you can purchase the Robinhood Gold service, which doubles your buying power and provides access to after-hours trading. Also, the app collects interest on the cash and securities stored in your account, just like banks do. In exchange, you get free, real-time trading. It's a great service for beginners; however, it is far from a full-service trading platform. The app lacks analytics and educational tools, so you might want to use it together with other financial information apps, such as Bloomberg or Benzinga.

TRADING APPS, CONTINUED

↤ *Gold Tracker.* Investors who seek stability often tend to look for commodities. Thus tangible assets such as gold, silver, or platinum become attractive investing options. If you are one of those people who seek a greater sense of control or simply want to diversify your portfolio, Gold Tracker may come in handy. It is exclusively an iOS app that helps to manage your precious metal resources with a clean user interface. It costs $2.99 and is available in the app store.

↤ *Openfolio.* This free digital financial assistant lets you quickly oversee the current state of your finances. It allows you to bring all your financial accounts in one place, including bank, brokerage, and other investment accounts. The app also equips you with smart insights, tips, forecasts, and tracking along with a holistic view of all your financial affairs.

↤ *Betterment.* If you're looking for an excellent robo-advisor for young investors, try Betterment. You can start with as little as $1 with a simple digital plan. Betterment seeks to minimize investment risks and maximize the returns. All you need to do is state your income and goals. Afterward, Betterment's award-winning portfolio management system does everything for you. So, if you do not have much time to get involved with investing, it might be the right option for you. The service charges a 0.25 percent annual fee and 0.40 percent commission for premium accounts with more than $100,000.

↤ *FeeX.* Just like its inspiration, the self-proclaimed "Robin Hood of fees" is on a noble mission to take from the rich and give to the poor. If you have an old 401(k) or IRA, you might want to check this one out. FeeX checks all your commission

TRADING APPS, CONTINUED

fees and helps you find ways to reduce them. The best part is that FeeX is absolutely free. If it manages to reduce your costs, FeeX earns its share via referral agreements with other financial service providers, so essentially it is a win-win for everyone.

- *SigFig.* This is another robo-advisor service. It has the highest starting investment level on this list, as it offers customized portfolios starting at $2,000. However, it has its benefits. SigFig streamlines the process of investing, so all you need to do is enter your age, investment period, income information, and risk level, and you will get a recommended portfolio that fits your needs. Also, it offers portfolio tracking and personalized human advice for free. So, you can use it even before you fund your SigFig account. It only charges the accounts with more than $10,000. The annual rate is 0.25 percent. Accounts between $2,000 and $10,000 are managed free of charge.

- *Wealthfront.* One of the best robo-advisors in the market, Wealthfront is designed to make investing simple and profitable. It's a superior service for young investors who prefer hands-off asset management. Also, it offers many handy features, such as financial planning, tax-loss harvesting, direct indexing, and free portfolio reviews. To start with Wealthfront, you need a $500 initial investment, and your first $10,000 is managed without any fee. For larger sums, the standard fee of 0.25 percent applies.

- *WiseBanyan.* A one-of-a-kind robo-advisor, WiseBanyan requires only $1 to start. More important, it does not charge any annual fees. Therefore, all its basic services are entirely complimentary. WiseBanyan makes money by

TRADING APPS, CONTINUED

selling personalized solutions for individual investors. The company firmly believes in financial empowerment and that investment future holds no extra costs.

❧ *Estimize*. A financial estimate service based on the wisdom of the crowd may not sound smart, but it has already proved to be more accurate than Wall Street 74 percent of the time. Estimize crowdsources insights from almost 60,000 analysts and reports on more than 2,000 stocks per quarter. In that way, the platform can produce unbiased and more accurate financial predictions. You can use Estimize to forecast the profits of your portfolio. The website provides estimates for particular stocks that you can use for your investment decisions. Registration is free, so everyone can join and contribute their expertise.

WHAT TO EXPECT WHEN YOU'RE INVESTING

To build passive income from the stock market, you need to look for consistency above all. You need stocks that will pay a worthwhile dividend regardless of whether the price goes up or down. Does that seem like a lot to ask? It shouldn't, because many stocks fit that description. Since they've always brought a good return on investment, there's reason to believe they always will. They're like good singles or doubles hitters on a baseball team. You can win a lot of games with them. They may not hit as many home runs as Babe Ruth, but as everyone knows, Babe Ruth also struck out more than any player in history. And you can't afford a lot of strikeouts when building passive income is your goal.

Once again, this is a matter of psychology. Much of our society is built on instant gratification. Highly motivated people are trained to have high expectations of themselves. They want a lot, and they want it right away. This includes stock market investors, who generally expect far too much—and who also expect it far too soon.

Consider an analogy to make this clear. As everyone knows, predicting the weather is difficult. You read the forecast for tomorrow, and you learn that there's going to be rain. But then the sun shines for the whole day. This happens because the weather is a chaotic system—and the shorter the time frame, the greater the chaos will be. If you're watching droplets of water slide down a window pane, you can reliably predict that the droplets will eventually reach the bottom, but you can't predict how long it will take them to get there or how many twists and turns they'll take along the way. There's long-term reliability, but there's also short-term randomness.

In the same way, you can make a distinction between weather and climate. If you live in Chicago, you can be sure that the month of January will be colder than the month of July. That's a matter of climate. But you can't be sure that the 10th of January will be colder than the 11th. Once again, the more you compress the time, the more room you make for confusion.

Consider Warren Buffett, one of the all-time most successful stock investors and also one of the wealthiest people in the world. Buffett has a very simple definition of investing: It's laying out money now to get more money back in the future. But what is the future? Is it tomorrow, or is it ten years from now? Needless to say, both are the future—but we need to focus on the long-term future to reap the immediate but small-scale gains that define passive income.

A BIT OF HISTORY

To see why this is so important, let's get some historical perspective. Specifically, try to think of all the things that happened between 1964 and 1981. There was the first moon landing, the war in Vietnam, the Watergate scandal, the arrival of the Beatles, the very different presidencies of Jimmy Carter and Ronald Reagan, and much more. There were also many changes in the economy, including runaway inflation and the gasoline crisis of the 1970s. Still, gross domestic product (GDP) in the United States—that is, the volume of all business being done in the country—rose by 370 percent. The overall sales of the Fortune 500 companies multiplied more than six times. And what happened to the stock market? Well, on December 31, 1964, the Dow Jones Industrial Average stood at 874. And on December 31, 1981, it stood at 875—a move of exactly one point. If you had bought a mutual fund that was indexed to the Dow, you might have been quite a frustrated investor. On the other hand, if you doggedly held onto your fund shares until 2018, you might be the very opposite of frustrated because as of this writing, the Dow is close to 25,000.

By now, you probably see how different segments of the economy seem to operate independently of each other. You'd think that a metric like the Dow Jones Average would keep pace with the GDP, but it didn't happen. The same kind of disconnect also happens within individual industries.

The automobile business is a case in point. During the 20th century, cars had an incredible effect on every aspect of American life. At one time, almost 20 percent of our total work force was in one way or another employed in the automotive industry. If you had known all this in the year 1900, you would have thought that you had found the key to the mint. Just invest in the car business, and you couldn't miss.

But let's look a bit closer. It may surprise you to learn that more than 2,000 makes of American cars came into being between 1900 and 1999, and virtually all of them failed. At the end of the 20th century only GM, Chrysler, and Ford were still making cars in the United States. So, if you had picked a car company as an investment at the beginning of the century, the odds are overwhelming that you would have lost your money despite the fact that cars literally transformed our way of life.

Regarding this, Warren Buffett once made a very insightful comment. Instead of betting on the success of car companies, an investor in 1900 would have done much better betting on the failure of horses. There were 21 million horses in the United States at the start of the 20th century, and at the end there were less than a quarter of that number. So, while it's true that only a few car companies made it through the century, virtually all the buggy whip and carriage companies went broke. But did anybody think of betting against the carriage makers, or "selling short," as it's known on Wall Street? Apparently not, because they'd have gotten so rich that we'd certainly know who they were.

The bottom line is, picking stocks as an investment can be exciting—but it's also very much a matter of chance, even for the most sophisticated buyers. If your primary interest is passive income, the best course is to look at the dividend histories of some companies and mutual funds. Then put your money into the strongest ones. Use the income to buy the financial freedom that is the goal of the passive income lifestyle, while perhaps reinvesting a portion of it as well.

On the other hand, if you want to balance passive income with a need for some excitement and action, that is also a legitimate choice. But you'll be a lot better off if you can avoid the most common mistakes that millions of independent investors make every single day.

CHAPTER SIX

LEVELING UP YOUR INVESTING GAME

Now that you've wrapped your mind around your "why," what type of investor you are, and some of the basic tenets of getting started in investing, it's time to dig deeper into some of the options you will have for investing beyond the traditional mutual fund route. In this chapter, we will sometimes adopt the viewpoint of a rather more ace investor than you might expect in a program on passive income. But remember: Passive income is not an end in itself. The goal of passive income is to bring you financial freedom—and if you decide to exercise some of that freedom by investing in stocks, you'll find some valuable information in this chapter. If you're not inclined toward becoming actively involved in the stock market, you can still generate passive income from stocks by buying dividend-producing securities. As you read in the previous chapter, these include mutual funds. But you may be interested in a reasonable amount of action as well as a certain amount of income, too.

As you're going to see, sometimes the key to doing something right is not doing something wrong. So, let's dig into some of the most common mistakes made by independent investors not only in buying stocks, but also in selling them. We'll start with some long-term strategic sources of error, and then we'll home in on the tactical mistakes that are made many thousands of times every day.

SET CLEAR GOALS

First, it's important to understand that this chapter is much more than a list of everything that can go wrong. Each of the mistakes you'll read about has a positive flip side that can translate into profit. For example, the first and perhaps most common error is investing without a clear goal in mind. It's easy to say, "Well, my goal is making money," but that was also your goal when you sold lemonade on the corner, and the stock market is a much more complicated game. So, think carefully about what you want from your investments, not only financially, but emotionally as well. Rremember your "why." If your main interest is consistent income and security, are you ready to completely turn your money over to a mutual fund manager? If you want to retain more control, how much risk are you willing to take on?

As you define your goals, be sure to attach a time frame. Be clear about how long you'll give yourself to accomplish the goals and when you'll want to re-evaluate them. For instance, if a year goes by and you're not happy with your mutual fund, don't just let it keep going by force of inertia. On a certain date, plan to take another look at what an investment is bringing you. Is it accomplishing the goal you bought it for? Or maybe your goals have changed. If that seems to be happening, make sure it's not because you've gotten bored with your goals and your plan for attaining them. Patience is one of the true keys to investment success. If you lack patience, you'll change direction too frequently and for the wrong reason. Many investors take a short-term view—even though they tell themselves they have long-term objectives. In the end, knowing your goals could mean making frequent changes in your portfolio—or perhaps making changes only rarely. The main thing is to make every decision a conscious one, and that starts with deciding what you really want to accomplish.

CHECK EMOTION AT THE DOOR

In the process of defining their goals, many investors focus on what the market might do, and they don't pay enough attention to how that will make them feel. Not allowing for the emotions that market cycles cause is our second big mistake. When things are going well, it's amazingly easy to believe you're a financial genius. And if you actually are a financial genius, it's even easier to think that you're the master of the universe. This was what happened several years ago to a stock market fund called Long Term Capital Management. It was founded by a number of truly brilliant academic economists who felt that they had a foolproof method of stock market investing. For a while the system worked great, and it attracted billions of dollars of investors' money.

The problem was, almost any system would have worked great at that time, because the market as a whole was in a bullish phase. But when the momentum shifted, the fund managers found it difficult to come down from the high they'd enjoyed for several years. They'd come to love that feeling, so that anything else seemed intolerable. What's more, the investing public had enjoyed believing in the existence of these invincible financial geniuses. In the end, the failure of Long Term Capital Management was such a shock that it almost caused a full-scale market crash. And the reason was very simple. The overblown optimism investors had felt very quickly translated into overblown fear. Unrealistic emotions have a way of doing that—so be aware of your feelings, and make sure they're in sync with reality.

AVOID INVESTMENT FADS

Investing in the latest fad or speculative trend is mistake number three. A great example was a stock called Pets.com. This company sold pet supplies over the internet, and it was the poster child for hype during the dotcom boom. Even Jeff Bezos, the CEO of Amazon, confessed that he had invested in Pets.com, and he admitted that it was one of his biggest mistakes. What happened to Jeff Bezos happened to a lot of people. They got carried away by the publicity—and by a stock price that grew daily—at least for a while. Within nine months of its first appearance on the New York Stock Exchange, Pets.com was worth nothing. So, when you see a rocketing stock price and all you hear is about this hot new company, think of this as warning signs, not buying signals.

Here's an easy way to remember that advice. Put the fingers of your right hand straight out and together. Then hold the hand in front of your face so you're looking at the palm. On the extreme left of your hand is your little finger, your pinky. This can represent the price of a stock when it first comes to your attention. It's pretty low, so you're not very interested. But look what happens next. There's your ring finger representing a significant rise in the stock price. Now you're watching more closely. Lots of people must be buying this stock. Maybe it's a real trend, something you wouldn't want to miss. In fact, the next time you check the stock price it's even higher, just like your middle finger is the longest one on your hand. You decide not to wait one more moment. You buy the stock at its all-time high, because you're convinced it's going to keep going up. After all, it's done nothing but go up since you first started watching it, right? But look at the next finger on your hand. It's your ring finger. It's shorter than your middle finger, and this symbolizes a decline in the stock price. How could this happen when there seemed to be so much upward momentum? You're a bit worried at this reversal, but you don't want to be a wimp. You decide to hold onto the stock and wait for the trend to turn positive again. Except now, look at your thumb. This is a sudden and precipitous drop in the stock price. At the sight of this, all the excitement you felt just a little while ago suddenly turns to gloom and doom. You're so miserable that you sell the stock even though it means taking a huge loss.

Could it be that the length of our fingers represents some sort of divinely given message about stock market investing? We don't need to answer that question, but there's no doubt the sequence we've just described is exactly what happens to a vast number of independent investors. It's exactly what happens when you let trend-spotting take over your stock-picking, and to make it even worse, most people don't even learn from their mistake. Maybe that's why we were given two hands.

Save Your Pennies

Since we're talking about the dangers of trendy investments, a related category of stocks bears mentioning as a prime example of a trend to be wary of—penny stocks. A *penny stock* is a stock valued at under $5 per share, which makes it highly speculative. With their low prices, penny stocks look like attractive bets, but there are several serious problems with this type of investment. First, you are betting that the price of the shares will rise, which for the purposes of passive income is always a bad idea. Second, in order to have even a chance of making money, you need to be trading a high volume of shares, which means the transaction fees will be high. And penny stocks are also more susceptible to fraud and manipulation. Your transactions may be perfectly legitimate, but you shouldn't ignore the fact that there have been many white-collar crime convictions in the world of penny stocks.

Be aware that in the age of the internet where anyone can claim to be an expert, getting hooked by trends is easier than ever. Remember the brother-in-law strategy of investing? The internet is like the ultimate brother-in-law investment guide. It's full of information, and well-designed websites can make even foolish ideas seem convincing. But the internet won't pay you back if its advice goes sour. It can be a good source of information, but treat it like your brother-in-law, not a trusted parent.

PUT DIVIDENDS IN PERSPECTIVE

When publicly held companies are profitable, they are obligated to share the profits with stockholders through quarterly payments called dividends. The more shares you own, the bigger your quarterly check will be. Dividends are a great way to build passive income through stocks. But as you look for investments that pay solid dividends, be sure to have a long-term perspective. Many inexperienced investors go hunting for dividends to get a quick return on their money, and this is almost always a mistake.

Here's why. When a stock is about to pay a dividend, the news is not a surprise to well-informed investors—including the big institutional funds. As a result, the amount of the anticipated dividend is almost reflected in the stock price before the dividend is paid out. That means you're paying more for the stock, and the increased price will, of course, detract from what you net out through the dividend. In other words, shopping for dividends means you're overpaying.

It's good to have dividend stocks in your portfolio (utility stocks are especially reliable) but they're not the only way of building passive income. Unless you're 100 percent risk-averse, a mixed portfolio makes more sense. Some of your stocks will almost certainly pay a dividend, but a few others might not do so for a long time, if ever. But if you do your research and buy carefully, you may get some blue chip stocks of the future at bargain prices. If and when those stocks do pay dividends, that money will be pure profit. It won't have been already built into the price you originally paid for the shares.

UNDERSTAND EARNINGS REPORTS

A similar mistake to hunting for dividends is giving too much weight to earnings reports—especially just before a new one is about to come out. As with dividends, the market will anticipate what the earnings report is going to show. That positive anticipation will be built into the share price, probably long before you even think of buying it. So even a really good earnings report is unlikely to catch anyone by surprise. Since most companies meet or beat expectations, this isn't news to anyone except real newbies in the market. Even if you are one of those newbies, don't make it obvious by buying into a positive earnings report.

In fact, you might be better off looking at a company that *doesn't* meet its earnings expectations. Do some research on why this happened. Does it look like management can rectify the situation? If that's your impression, the stock might be a good long-term investment. Meanwhile, the stock price will likely go down, which could create an even more attractive opportunity.

Always be aware that high and low are relative terms in the stock market. Three hundred may seem like too much for a stock, while $3 might seem like a bargain. But you have to put the price in context. What are the basic strengths and weaknesses of a company? Are these accurately reflected in the stock price, or is the market making a mistake? And the market doesn't make too many mistakes, at least not for very long. Just because a stock price is low, doesn't mean it's a good buy. And, conversely, just because the price is high, doesn't mean it's a bad buy. The mistake is not knowing that "buy low, sell high" is really shorthand for "buy stocks that are undervalued and sell stocks that are overvalued."

In the end, there's a good chance that the price you see for a stock is exactly what that stock is worth. So, don't assume that a stock is selling way too high or way too low. A much better assumption is that the millions of investors who are behind that price have seen something that you've missed.

AVOID GURU SYNDROME

Some small investors try to simplify these matters by just following the lead of well-known stock market gurus. The guru may be a writer or TV personality, or a large-scale investor like Warren Buffett. While a lot can be learned from people who have made millions in the market, your goals and motivations are bound to be very different, and you won't attain those goals by copying anyone else. The problem is, mirroring someone else's moves doesn't allow you to develop a real strategy of your own. Warren Buffet's investment strategy, for example, has obviously worked well for him over many years, but it's based on holding onto certain select stocks for long periods of time. Aside from making him a lot of money, this is the approach that makes him comfortable. But are you going to be comfortable just because he's comfortable? Moreover, Warren Buffett would be a difficult model to follow, because he very rarely makes a move. You'd probably want to model yourself on someone a bit more active, so you'd need to research the different stock market personalities. But if you're going to be doing that kind of research, you might as well just research the stocks themselves and make you own decisions.

A better course is to strike a balance between ignoring and imitating the stock market gurus. You can certainly follow what some of these investors are doing if only because they have the influence and the money to influence markets. But following in this sense means paying attention, not copying. Learn everything you can, but definitely learn to think for yourself.

AVOID THE FRIEND ZONE

Along the same lines of the brother-in-law investor you read about earlier, chances are you have friends with their own ideas about investments. Listen to what they have to say, but don't take anyone's advice at face value. That isn't to say their advice might not be good. They could be right. But find out where your friends get their information. If they have a broker that has made them a lot of money, ask for a referral. If they have their own strategy, ask them to teach it to you. You may decide to reject it, but you may also learn something in the process.

Sometimes friends also invoke the wisdom of others, and frequently, it's their stockbrokers. There are people who begin every sentence with "My broker says . . ." Well, who is this broker? Are they a stock market expert? That's quite possible. Do they have an agenda of their own? That's also quite possible. Essentially, a stockbroker is a salesperson. They are trying to sell you their services, which can only come into play when you buy or sell a stock. And with a broker, there's always one question that's difficult to answer: If they know so much about the stock market, why are they working for a brokerage house instead of playing in Warren Buffett's weekly bridge game? That may be an unfair question, but no one has the power to predict the future (not even the Oracle of Omaha), although we sometimes would like to believe differently.

INVESTING IS NOT A SPORT

Many of the investing mistakes we've been looking at so far can be summed up very simply. Many people make the basic error of confusing investing with sports. That's why people talk about "playing the stock market." They root for their stocks just like they root for their favorite teams. They idolize their favorite market gurus just like they love a great pitcher or quarterback. It all becomes emotional, especially when a stock starts going down. We ask ourselves, "Are we going to abandon that stock just because it goes into a slump? What kind of fans would that make us? Wouldn't there be something really disloyal about that?"

If you have thoughts like those, remind yourself that you're not a fan—you're an investor. Being an investor is partly an emotional experience, but it should never be a sentimental one. Success is a relative term when it comes to investing. Ideally, we think of success as making more money. But sometimes it's about losing less. If a stock goes into a decline and you can see a good reason why that's happening, you may need to cut your losses. A smart investor not only knows when a stock is in a tailspin, but immediately takes action to let it go. By the same token, a stock that is obviously undervalued shouldn't be overlooked.

A flip side of this is unwillingness to sell a stock that has gone up because you're afraid that it might go higher. Unfortunately, there is no easy answer for this. The best course is to examine your own motives. Are you tempted to make a move because of fear? That's usually not a good idea. Or are you tempted by greed? Are you going to let yourself feel disappointed in a small profit because you're imagining the big

SHOULD YOU DAY TRADE?

By Brian Hughes, *Entrepreneur* guest writer and CEO of
Integrity Marketing and Consulting

Is dabbling in day trading worth it? Most financial advisors would say no. Why? Day trading—buying and selling stocks rapidly over the course of a day—is time and resource intensive. Traditional investment advice says you are far better seeking solid, long-term performance opportunities than the quick rush of day trading. This advice isn't wrong, but it ignores the fact that some day traders do make a profit.

While the fast-paced action can be quite the rush at first, most folks who get into day trading lack the base knowledge and tools to be successful. As a result, roughly 80 percent of day traders end up in the red, reports The Motley Fool. Additionally, since the IRS taxes day-trading profits at ordinary income tax rates rather than long-term capital gains, if you do make a profit, you'll end up handing a hefty chunk back to the IRS.

Day traders who want to make money look for stocks with high "betas." A beta quantifies how fast a stock can rise or fall within a given market. Essentially, these are businesses that are more volatile than the surrounding market. The Motley Fool did an analysis of common day trading stocks in 2014, looking specifically at betas to determine whether these stocks were a good investment. At the time, Weight Watchers, for example, had a beta of 3.34. This means that the stock could rise (or fall) 3.34 times as fast as the market, which is a significant jump over the normal movement of the market. Get in on the bottom of a fast rise then sell high, and you could make a lot of money very quickly. Day traders go after stocks like these that offer speedy gains, thanks to high trading volume.

SHOULD YOU DAY TRADE?, CONTINUED

Day traders also look at penny stocks. While the U.S. Securities and Exchange Commission (SEC) reports that penny stocks trade for $5 or less per share, due to high trading volume, these stocks can nonetheless lead to a big profit. Of course, a tremendous amount of research—and sheer luck—is involved in following this approach to day trading. The average American doesn't have the time to engage in the market this way, which is why investment professionals generally recommend the "slow and steady" approach to investing.

Let's say you invested $10,000 in Texas Instruments or Pfizer 20 years ago. Today, those investments would be worth $145,700 and $113,400, respectively. Invest $10,000 in day trading, and you might end up with nothing. Then again, had you invested in a company like Eastman Kodak, your $10,000 would have evaporated to $3,500. There's risk with every investment!

Recently, binary options have been taking the day trading world by storm, diversifying portfolios with this new high-return investment. Binary options are replacing Forex (a decentralized global market where all the world's currencies are traded) as a hot trading option.

Binary options are a financial investment tool day traders use to hold a position on the future direction of an asset, like a stock, commodity, or currency exchange rate. In short, a binary option is a way to "place a bet" that the value of the asset in question will increase or decrease. Investors don't actually own the underlying asset.

To trade binary options, you'll need to use a trading platform. Look for platforms that are broker-regulated, offer a range of underlying assets, and have real customer reviews. While you can't make everyone happy all the time, a trustworthy and reliable platform should have an abundance of positive reviews.

SHOULD YOU DAY TRADE?, CONTINUED

While there's certainly a big risk involved in day trading, binary options trading or even Forex trading are two ways to get involved with less risk. If you don't have the time to be intensely involved with trading, day trading is probably not for you. But if you're considering a new option for fast gains, binary-options trading strategies are worth investigating further. Before getting started, consider setting up a practice account to learn the ropes without losing any cash.

one that might get away? There are so many ways to talk yourself into or out of almost anything, especially when it comes to investments. But what you really need is this: Stay disciplined, don't be greedy, and don't be scared, either.

If you become emotionally attached to your stocks, you'll end up paying with losses. Part of the reason good investors fall prey to this trap is that they put so much work into finding the "right" stock. They read books on investing, devise stock-picking systems, and scrutinize earnings reports and market trends. Finally, the investor narrows his or her choice down to one special "gem." But if you let this stock become your pride and joy (your child, as it were), you may suffer grave losses for it. The fact is, emotional attachment to stocks is nothing more than human nature—and wanting to be right. But do you want to be right and also broke?

BE AWARE OF MARKET CONDITIONS

Another problem is, the market doesn't send out an email when conditions change. You have to pay attention on a day-to-day basis. But in order to follow your investments closely, be prepared to put in the time that's required. If you're not so inclined, stick to mutual funds where you'll only have to review things on a quarterly basis. If you're using the services of a brokerage house, you can also program your stocks to sell automatically if certain high or low prices are reached. But be aware that there is a fee for every transaction, whether it's automatic or not. And those fees can add up.

Generally speaking, the economy moves in cycles. So, does the stock market. Upward trends are followed by downward trends. Of course, everybody wants to buy stocks during boom years, but finding investors in a bear market can be like pulling teeth. Yet there are more bargain investments in leaner times. Staying out of the market in those years can be a big mistake.

KNOW WHEN TO FOLD 'EM

For the most part, we've devoted this chapter to buying decisions. But the only thing harder than buying a stock is deciding when to sell. To conclude this chapter, we'll focus on some simple guidelines for helping you decide whether to sell a stock. Whether you need to cut your losses or take a profit, please pay close attention.

Many investors find it hard to sell a stock, especially if it's a strong company providing some good passive income. But very few stocks exist outside the influence of the market as a whole or even of a segment of the market. More often than not, a good stock that's performing badly is in a sector that's performing badly.

History is a great teacher of this principle: When a down market occurred following the dotcom boom, the technology sector as a whole was hit hard. It wasn't just stocks with massive debt and no income. Profitable companies with solid business structures were devalued as well. But here's the really hard lesson: In many cases, people who held on to tech companies are still waiting for those stocks to return their losses. And it's been more than ten years.

If you own a stock in a sector that is being battered, even a good stock, you should almost definitely sell, because even good companies aren't safe from the power of a strong downward pull. Never forget Warren Buffet's number-one principle of successful stock market investing: Don't lose money!

And if one of your stocks is going up, remember that a profit doesn't exist until you've taken your money off the table. Despite this obvious fact, many investors like to inflate their egos by viewing their stocks online and relishing how much money they've made. In reality, you haven't made a penny until you press the "sell" button. So, don't be afraid to push it.

When a stock is suddenly spiking upward, you may sense it's out of control. The price-earnings ratio becomes very inflated, media attention may start up, and you begin to wonder just how much higher it can possibly go. Stop wondering and sell at least part of your investment—perhaps one-third or a half of what you own. That way, you can take some profit off the table and still keep yourself in the game. If your stock does hit the moon, you won't be left kicking yourself for selling completely out of your position.

The real secret to knowing when to sell is to keep yourself as well informed as you possibly can. Nothing influences the stock market more than the news. Read the *Wall Street Journal*, read the business section of the *New York Times*, read investment sites on the internet, and then read some more. Keeping informed is like buying insurance: The more information you have, the more you're protected.

Summing up, no aspect of stock market investing is an exact science. When it comes to knowing when to sell, there are only indicators that can give us clues. Learning from the mistakes of others is a great strategy for avoiding making those same mistakes yourself. If a solid company has a downward spiraling stock price, look for clues as to why and find out what is happening within that sector. Remember to keep a clear head when evaluating stocks and don't become emotionally attached to them. Finally, never forget that knowledge is powerful. Read the books of those who have been successfully trading and investing because they offer a wealth of knowledge and experience. There are many factors—perhaps *too* many factors—that affect the financial markets. But if you're willing to put in the time and effort to read and research your investments, you will be well prepared to take profits and avoid losses.

CHAPTER SEVEN

INVESTING IN REAL ESTATE

You've already read about moves you can make to earn a passive income online and in the stock market. Now we're going to see how you can achieve the same goal in what is probably the most time-honored medium of all. Long-term real estate investment has always been an outstanding business opportunity and the basic reason is very simple. As someone once said, "They aren't making any more land." For that reason, real estate is a great investment to hold. Like any market, there can be fluctuations, but in the long run, land retains its value and usually increases as well.

For building passive income, your approach to real estate investment should be simple. It can be summed up in just a couple of points: focusing on one property and leveraging your assets. Each of these points, of course, could be the subject of a whole chapter in itself, but for now, we'll give just a brief explanation of each one. Once you get a sense of how passive investment from real estate actually works, much of what you're about to hear will be self-explanatory.

START SINGLE

First, your immediate goal is to gain control of one single family home. We're not going to be dealing with commercial properties. You're not going to look at any duplexes or apartment buildings. Just a single-family home in a solid neighborhood, not an affluent neighborhood, and not a struggling neighborhood. Why? Because you're going to rent it out. So, to begin, you're going to use some of your leisure time to scout out various areas that you might be interested in. If you see a house with a "For Sale" sign and it looks interesting, write down the address, but don't even think about making an offer until you've looked at a half-dozen different neighborhoods at least.

When you've found a neighborhood and a single-family dwelling that looks good, be aware that this property—or some property like it—will be your *only* purchase for at least one year. This is an extremely critical point. You are going to acquire only one property, and you are going to make the smallest possible down payment you possibly can. Ideally, you will make no down payment at all. Then you will rent out the property at a rate that will cover your mortgage payments and your other expenses.

Once these costs are covered, you can devote whatever is left over to passive income. The amount of this passive income will increase over time, but if you really want to get ahead as a real estate investor, you will spend little or any of this income at least for the first few years. Instead, you will save it in order to make a down payment on another property. And when you have that second property, the cycle can begin all over again. In this way, you can leverage control of the maximum number of properties with the smallest amount of cash outlay. For now, the most important thing is to identify the immediate goal. That goal is to find a solid neighborhood, then find a good, single-family home in that neighborhood, and use the rent to maintain the property and to generate some income. Then, when the time is right, you can use that income to get control of another house.

LEVERAGE FOR THE WIN

Even without the income stream, you can make money simply by the innate power of real estate to stay ahead of inflation and by the power of smart leveraging of your assets. For example, say you buy a property today for $100,000 cash. It may appreciate in value 5 percent a year for 10 years, during a time when inflation averages only 3 percent. If this happens, the property will be worth over $163,000, when another investment that matched the inflation rate would only be worth about $135,000. Your real estate investment would have beaten inflation by $28,000. But if you had put the $100,000 under your mattress, your cash would only buy about 65 percent of what it will buy today.

But here's what makes leveraging so powerful. What if instead of paying cash, you paid only 10 percent down and financed the balance? You would start with $10,000 in equity. If you rented the property so that your tenants covered all your expenses, in ten years, your $10,000 equity would have grown to $73,000—and that's before you add the thousands of dollars by which the mortgage was paid down. If it only paid down $27,000, your equity would be $100,000, or 1,000 percent of your initial $10,000 investment.

At first, the mortgage reduction will be small, maybe only a few dollars per month per property. This doesn't seem like much, but considering that it's every month, on every property you own, it starts to add up quickly. In addition, with each payment you make, the amount that goes toward reducing the mortgage goes up and the interest goes down. Every month you own the property, more of the payment goes to reducing the mortgage until the mortgage is fully paid.

The beauty of it is that the higher the inflation rate, the greater your growth in value. But there's still more. While the value of the property is going up, so is the monthly rent. As the rent increases and the mortgage pays down, you start enjoying the passive income flow this produces.

As you learn how to make all this happen, remember that we're talking about investment, not speculation. Your focus should be on finding good properties that will pay for themselves and generate income. There are a lot of get-rich-quick schemes in real estate, but this isn't one of them. Remember: First and foremost, your goal is to create freedom. You want to get yourself out of the money-for-time trap that forces you to play financial defense year after year. When you are the owner of six or eight self-sustaining rental properties, you will achieve that goal.

All of this takes patience, but it doesn't take a lot of money. It doesn't even take a lot of hard work. Discipline and commitment are much more important. That's why real estate is such a great investment opportunity, and that's also why more people don't take advantage of it. They're in too big of a hurry. They give up too quickly. They're still trying to trade their time and their labor to become wealthy, and that trade just doesn't work anymore. So, they become discouraged and quit.

Let Others Leverage for You

When you follow a passive income real estate strategy, you're not leveraging your own money and labor—you're leveraging the assets of the people who rent your properties. Those people are actually helping you become wealthy. When you own rental properties, you create a downline of tenants who go to work for someone else and earn money to pay off your mortgages. It may sound insensitive, but that's the way the system works, and anyone who doesn't take advantage of it is missing a great opportunity. And that applies to *anyone*, because real estate investing isn't limited to wealthy tycoons. The truth is, more often than not, real estate is how those tycoons became wealthy in the first place. Andrew Carnegie, one of the richest men in the world, made exactly this point when he said, "Ninety percent of all millionaires became so through owning real estate. More money has been made in real estate than in all industrial investments. A smart wage earner today invests his paycheck in real estate."

When you make that investment, instead of being a slave to a weekly paycheck, you provide a way for other people to help you get rich. Even if you only buy one rental house a year, each purchase allows you to benefit from the labor of another person, and this will eventually make you rich. It won't happen overnight, but slowly and surely it will happen. It always has, and it always will.

It's just a matter of remembering that buying right is far more important that buying often. It's seeing why the income stream your properties generate is far more important than the number of properties you own. And to ensure that your income stream keeps coming, you need to be aware that the price you pay for a property is not nearly as important as the cost of owning it. By keeping that cost low, you can turn a trickle of income into a flood by raising rents only a small amount each year. And one of the best ways to keep those costs down is by paying for them with something else: your sweat.

SWEAT EQUITY: WORTH THE COST?

Sweat equity is exactly what it sounds like. Instead of putting hard cash into your investment property, you are paying with your own labor. For example, instead of paying a contractor to paint your rental house, you might do it yourself. Instead of hiring someone to tile the kitchen backsplash, you watch a few YouTube videos and DIY it for half the cost. Sweat equity can have the potential to pay good dividends, but keep in mind that it doesn't really help you have a passive income stream since there's nothing passive about sweating it out. Read about how that worked out for Laura, who has successfully made that journey, including some unexpected turns in the road.

> *When I began to think about real estate investing, there was one thing that really attracted me. It was the fact that, at least in theory, a person could start controlling property with little or no money at*

the outset. I had heard the stories of people getting rich with no down payment on their purchases, and that really appealed to me—because I couldn't have made a down payment even if I'd wanted to.

Here's what I very quickly learned. There is actually more than one kind of down payment. Or to put it another way, there are two kinds of equity that you can invest in a piece of property. One is plain old hard currency. You go to the bank for a loan, and they ask you how much cash you can put up. The more you have, the better you look to a banker. But I was surprised to learn that making a substantial down payment is not the only thing lenders look for. It's not even the most important thing. There's another kind of equity investment that's even more attractive than cash. It's not cash equity, it's sweat equity. Sweat equity is a term I had never heard before I started trying to buy property, but having it is the reason that many people succeed in real estate—and not having it is the reason many people fail.

In the fewest possible words, sweat equity is the amount of work you put into developing your property. You may not have money, but if you can convince a lender that you're going to knock yourself out improving the fixer-upper you want, the lender may very well give you what you want. That's because your hard work is not only going to raise the value of your individual property, but it will raise the value of the entire community. And after all, it's the community that the lender really cares about. If there are enough people like you putting sweat equity into their buildings, the outcome is bound to be good. That's why your sweat equity will almost always be more attractive than someone else's cash.

In terms of passive income, that story is something of a mixed message. On the one hand, it's good news that you can become a real estate investor with little or no money. The "no money down" route to success has been much talked about, and it really does exist. For the purposes of this program, however, sweat equity as an alternative to financial capital is not really workable. That's because our goal here is not working harder and longer—even if it eventually brings increased income. Our definition of wealth is financial freedom based on passive income streams. Toward that end, you're going to learn to buy property so that it shows a cash flow right from the start. The flow will be only a few drops at the very start, but it will grow into a rising tide—and there's even a real chance that it may turn into a genuine flood of wealth.

INVESTMENT VS. SPECULATION

Of course, once you have financial freedom, you can choose to do whatever you want with it. You can even work harder than ever. However, that should be a choice rather than a necessity. Because the truth is, you don't have to work yourself to the bone to generate passive income through real estate investment. But remember: We're making a sharp distinction here between investment and speculation. But what are the real differences? Well, one difference is the role of time. For a speculator, a quick payoff is an important goal. A good example of real estate speculation is house flipping. The speculator buys a property, renovates it, and then sells it as quickly as possible. Depending on the kind of renovation, the whole process can take 90 days or less. That's the goal, anyway. If there's a downturn in the market, however, speculators can get stuck with renovated properties that no one is prepared to buy. And since they're speculators rather than investors, they're not prepared to rent out the property and create an income stream. They wanted a quick payoff, and they were willing to work very hard for a concentrated period of time. If the payoff comes, the speculation was successful. If the payoff doesn't come, or doesn't come quickly, the speculation failed.

To build passive income through real estate, you're going to be an investor rather than a speculator. That means you're going to take your time. You're not going to be in a hurry. When the market is hot and prices are going up, you're not going to get caught up the euphoria and pay too much. When the market cools off and prices fall, you're not going to sell in a panic because you're afraid prices will go down even more.

Plenty of real estate gurus will urge you to buy all the property you can. The idea is that it will go up in value and you'll get rich when you sell. But what if it doesn't go up in value? What if you can't sell your property because there's nobody who wants to buy it? A real estate investor, as opposed to a speculator, never has to face those problems. Real estate investors never *have* to sell their properties. They may *choose* to sell, but they're never forced to because they never depend on the value rising.

FIND PROPERTIES THAT FIT YOUR GOALS

When you first start thinking seriously about investing in real estate, two thoughts are certain to enter your mind: How can you find good properties to invest in, and how can you make the best possible deal for those properties?

For some insight on those questions, let's meet a real estate investor, Catherine, who solved them for herself—and who created major passive income in the process:

I got interested in real estate because it seemed like a solid investment in the literal sense. I wanted something I could see and put my hands on, not just a symbol like a stock certificate or a bond. Since I was a complete novice, I started out by reading books and attending a few seminars. And I quickly noticed one thing. Almost all the experts stressed the importance of finding properties that were not only well-built structures, but that could be acquired under the most favorable terms possible. In the years since then, I've bought a number of properties and I've come close to buying many more. In terms of finding good properties, I've found that certain strategies work much better than others. By following the most effective strategies, you can save yourself a lot of work—and possibly make yourself some very good money.

I wish I could tell you that there's some secret source of great properties that you can tap into right away. Actually, if I knew a secret like that I would probably keep it to myself—but there's no point in wondering about that, because there are no secrets in finding good properties. And in a way, that's a secret in itself—because some of the best properties are right out there in the open, hiding in plain sight.

The MLS

The Multiple Listing Service (MLS) is a good example of this. The MLS is a catalog of all the properties listed for sale by brokers in your area. There are hundreds and hundreds of properties. Some of them are good deals for investors and some aren't. The trick is to ferret out which properties have motivated sellers without making offers on all of them. With a lot of practice, you can see through agent jargon like "handyman's special" and "fixer-upper." That means the property looks bad, smells bad, and has at least one major system that doesn't function. And that almost always means it deserves a closer look. You don't want to buy a house if it's in total disrepair, but you also don't want to limit yourself to properties that can only get worse. So those kinds of properties are often a good starting point. In other words, the MLS can work well enough that you might find yourself, more often than not, in the market for really ugly properties. Coincidentally, these are the same properties that most agents prefer not to spend a lot of time with. In many cases, they're very cooperative—particularly, if you're in a position to offer cash and a quick closing.

One really good thing about properties in the MLS is that you know they're actually for sale. This may seem like an obvious statement, but compare it to some of the other methods touted as great ways to find deals. They involve locating owners, then finding out if they want to sell, and sometimes convincing them to sell even if they don't immediately want to. Properties in the MLS also have the advantage that all the information is pretty much laid out for you. That's a major time saver. It's only a matter of a few keystrokes to view all the properties that a broker has to offer—everything from handyman's specials to fine homes that are in move-in condition.

Alternate Property Strategies

Compared to the MLS, some other strategies can be much less effective. Here, again, is Catherine:

> When I first got into real estate, I was very aggressive. I decided to initiate a direct mail campaign to real estate agents. I was hoping that I might be able to find MLS-listed properties even before the listings became public. All I had to do was let agents know what I was looking for. So, I bought a thousand agent names from the Board of Realtors and created a three-part mailing to send to every one of them.
>
> The theme of my mailing was this: If you, my dear broker, have a property listed that fits my criteria, I'll make an offer and you get to keep the entire commission. I sent out my first thousand letters, all mailed first class, and the phone calls came rolling in—all seven of them, and that was all. The week after the letters went out, I got seven calls, four of which were good properties but out of my price range, and three were overpriced listings about to expire.
>
> My second mailing generated more results—about 15 calls—but all were basically in the same categories. The final mailing, a postcard, received no response at all. Basically, I wasted about $1,400 on a campaign that generated absolutely nothing.

As Catherine's story shows, the idea of mailing to brokers has some merit, but with some important tweaks. First, you should target only the 200 or so agents who list the types of properties you buy. Second, you can do a better job of writing the letters, emphasizing how the agent and their seller would benefit from working with you. Third, make your campaign a continuous one throughout the year, testing different letters for response and mailing the best to the same agents over and over. And lastly, you can personalize the campaign by following up with a phone call to the 50 best prospects.

PARTING THOUGHTS

In this chapter, we've made three very important points. First, we're going to measure your success as a real estate investor in terms of passive income streams. We're not going to focus on how many properties you own or how quickly you can turn them around.

Secondly, we're not going to buy properties in the hope that they'll go up in value. The truth is, they almost certainly will over the long term, but that doesn't need to happen in order to generate income. Regardless of what the market is like at a given moment, you can always invest your income in upgrading your properties. New carpet, new windows, and new siding and air conditioning are all wise improvements that will enable you to raise your rent, increase your cash flow, and consistently improve your property. And even when the value of a property does increase, you may choose not to sell it because the passive income stream is so powerful.

Finally, this isn't about generating sweat equity. You're not going to be working harder and harder to make up for a lack of capital. In fact, the most work you're going to do will be scouting around for properties and negotiating the right terms. Once you've taken control of a property, you'll be hiring a professional property manager, and that will be paid for by a percentage of the income from your property. If something in your property needs attention—whether it's a plumbing problem or electrical repair or anything else—your manager will be responsible for hiring someone to fix it. Passive income is more than just making money. It's more than just working hard. Lots of people are doing that. The problem is, they're not building real wealth. On the other hand, passive income from real estate is a great way to do just that.

CHAPTER EIGHT

LEVELING UP YOUR REAL ESTATE INVESTMENT STRATEGY

Once you get your footing in real estate through a single property, you can start to snowball your ownership and create multiple revenue streams. And once you do that, you can start to get a better feel for how to maximize your earning potential while managing the day-to-day operation of this income funnel with minimal maintenance. In this chapter, we're going to dig deeper into what it's actually like to own and invest in real estate. You'll see how the challenges, opportunities, and tricks of the trade play out in the real world. Most important, you'll learn more about why real estate is one of the most solid investments you can make—not just for passive income, but for long-term wealth and security. But before you can realize those long-term goals, you may need a quick reality check. Why? Because real estate isn't an instant-gratification formula for making money. Rather, it's a long-game strategy.

You already learned about the process of getting into real estate investing and acquiring your first property, patiently scouting out neighborhoods, and finding a single-family home for your first investment. Hundreds of thousands of people have gone through this process, and within six months of buying their first rental property, almost all those investors have the same reaction. It sounds something like this:

What's going on here? When does the money start rolling in? It seems like all I'm doing is paying bills, dealing with my tenants' complaints, and worrying about how I'm going to pay my property taxes. There are a million little things I never expected, and it seems like all of them cost money. At this point I'm barely breaking even.

When new real estate investors have feelings like these (and you *will* have some feelings like these), shoot for patience, even if it's hard. Remember, even if you're only breaking even after paying your bills, you're still paying down the mortgage every month, which is virtually the same thing as making a monthly deposit to a savings account. Moreover, time is on your side. As your rents rise with inflation, your passive income flow will start increasing each month—$25 more, then $50 more, and it will all begin to add up. Over the long term, as the mortgages are paid down on your property, more and more of the income will be yours. For you, that will mean prosperity, security, and overall financial freedom—which are what passive income is really all about.

THE GUIDING PRINCIPLES OF REAL ESTATE INVESTMENT

All of that is true even if you own only one property. But why stop there? Not buying at all is just as bad as buying too quickly. In fact, it gets much easier as you become a more experienced real estate investor. Just keep a few key principles in mind. Learn all you can about your local real estate market. Develop the ability to recognize solid properties and potentially good deals. And have the confidence to present and negotiate your offer to a seller. Those are the basics. But let's go beyond the basics and talk about five hands-on ideas that should always be in your mind as a real estate investor.

Put People First

First, never forget that houses, deals, and financing are only the tip of the iceberg. The essence of real estate, like any other business, is people. And every single buyer, seller, or renter you interact with is motivated by something different. While your main goal is making passive income, keep in mind that not every seller is motivated by money. Some, as you'll read below, have other goals in mind. Here's a real-life example of what that means. Take a look at Joan's story:

About six months into my real estate career, I made my first deal. The seller was an elderly lady named Dorothy, and she was very forceful in letting me know her feelings. She was convinced that she had been cheated in the past when she'd sold a house, and she was not going to let that happen again. Of course, I made it clear to her that I had no intention of trying to cheat her, and I was sure she knew that anyway. I suspected that her war stories were just a way of setting me up for some hard negotiating. So, I was surprised when Dorothy told me right up front that all she wanted for her home was the loan balance, plus $1,000 to move. There was no doubt that her property was worth much more than that, but Dorothy had a perfectly reasonable explanation. It seems that her husband had recently died, and she was going to live with her daughter and grandchildren. The bottom line was, she wanted to be gone by the end of the month. For her, that was the most important consideration.

Although this was my first actual deal, it wasn't my first attempt at a deal. Up to that point, I had made at least a hundred offers that had gotten nowhere. Like many new investors, I hadn't fully grasped the fact that real estate was about people, not properties; as a result, I had never really considered why an owner wanted to sell—and whether the price would be low or high. I just assumed their motives as sellers were the mirror image of mine as a buyer.

Dorothy taught me the all-important lesson that people don't nec-essarily want what you think they should want—and they don't necessarily act for the same reasons you do. Her house was in pretty good shape; she could have sold it for full value in 60 days or so. But what she wanted wasn't the top price. What she wanted was speed. She wasn't motivated by money, but by a desire to start a new phase of her life. She wanted to put her old life behind her, and her house was a symbol of her old life. With this in mind, Dorothy was per-fectly content to accept about a third less than the actual value of her property, provided the transaction could take place as soon as possible. That turned out to be exactly one week later.

Up to that point, Joan had assumed that anyone who owned a rundown house in a questionable neighborhood would be willing to sell cheap. She had also assumed that anyone with a nice house in a good neighborhood would be looking for top dollar. But what she learned from working with Dorothy could have saved the time and energy she put into all those fruitless offers. People are unique individuals, and sometimes the only way to really know what they want out of a deal is to ask them. So, if you're making offer after offer and getting rejection after rejection, you should think about talking to sellers about what they want, instead of assuming that you already know.

Keep Friendships Separate from Business

Once you've purchased a rental property, the next all-important step is finding a reliable tenant. To make this easier, here's a principle that will rule out a substantial number of applicants: Never rent to anyone you know.

You may still have a lot to learn about real estate, but there's one thing that is certain: Sooner or later your friend, your cousin, or the person you once talked to at a dinner party is going to be looking for a place to live—and they'll be looking at exactly the same time that you have a vacancy. It's going to seem like that this is a perfect solution for both of you. After all, your cousin Joe's a nice guy, and he even has some carpentry skills. He eagerly offers to do some work on your property and fix it up real nice. So, in a gesture that you will never cease to regret, you offer your vacant property to Joe. He gets a discounted rent because of the work he's going to do for you, and you get a tenant you can trust. Everybody wins, right?

Well, everybody wins except anyone who's even remotely involved in a situation like this. Here's the thing to keep in mind about renting to people you know: You and your friend or family member are entering the agreement with opposing views of the possible benefits. You as the property owner are happy because you know your buddy will treat you fairly—meaning that the rent will be on time, the repairs you agreed on will be made in a timely fashion, and he won't let the bathtub overflow. He goes in happy because he knows you'll treat him fairly, too—except to him that means you'll let him slide on the rent at Christmas, take his time on the repairs, and raise pit bulls in the basement. You think he'll be the perfect tenant; he thinks you'll be the perfect landlord. It's a conflict of viewpoints that isn't easily resolved, at least not without a lawyer.

When you become a real estate investor, your outlook on life undergoes a major change. Unless your friends are also property owners, they haven't experienced this kind of entrepreneurship. Chances are, they have no idea what it's like to invest huge chunks of time and money in a property. We've all heard the stories of the guy who lost not one but an entire group of college friends when he evicted one of them for nonpayment of rent. Suddenly, he became "the landlord," and he was no longer welcome at the softball games. Or there's the guy with a brother-in-law who can't see him at family gatherings without mentioning how shabbily he treated his best friend by forcing him to pay late fees every month.

The fact is, something is bound to go wrong in these scenarios. Very rarely do friend-to-tenant transformations work out to the satisfaction of both parties. On the bright side, since no one ever tells people that renting to friends and relatives is a bad thing, there are an awful lot of buying opportunities out there. They come into being when owners realize they're never going to see a dime out of Cousin Joe.

Take Your Guru with a Grain of Salt

Many new real estate investors have a mentor, or even a "guru" (similar to the investment guru you already read about, but more personally accessible). This is someone who provides not advice but a comprehensive worldview that helps to direct and focus the newcomer on a particular strategy. These gurus can take the form of a real estate professional, an academic instructor, or a family member who has experience in the business. One of the major attractions of these experts is their certainty that their particular strategy is the last word in real estate investing. But really, there is no last word. There is no single best way to develop passive income through property ownership. Instead, there are many ways, each of which can work well for a particular person in a specific situation. So take your guru with a grain of salt.

Let's say your father had success in real estate, and he was convinced it was because he never varied in his approach. He always bought houses for cash, then refinanced several of them as a package. Then he had more cash to buy more houses. No property—regardless of the type, condition, or location ever got any other treatment. And like most gurus, he was willing to defend his method to the death. He was certain that all other strategies were less profitable, more difficult to execute, and basically inferior to his special favorite. Yeah, sure—he's your dad. But you have an arsenal of knowledge at your fingertips. Do your own research, thank Dad for his opinion, and make your own decision.

Real estate gurus are compelling figures to new investors precisely because they are so focused and certain of themselves. Following a particular guru can be extremely valuable for overwhelmed novices, because it allows them to learn a particular technique in great depth. The downside is that guru-worship limits the new investor's experience. As a result, their followers tend to have a narrow viewpoint in terms of what a "good" deal is. This causes them to pass up some profitable opportunities.

Fully Vet Your Renters—No Exceptions

This final concept is absolutely essential to understand, but maybe not easy to accept. The fact is, people don't always tell the truth, especially where money is concerned.

Most of us grew up with the idea that lying was a bad thing to do. Furthermore, getting caught lying was embarrassing and could get you into a lot of trouble. But some people who apply to rent houses missed this lesson as kids—or maybe they unlearned it as adults. Either way, it's important to keep it in mind and ramp up your efforts to check the credentials and credit of potential renters. Otherwise, you may end up renting your houses to some really disappointing tenants. Here, Lily tells her story about finding out way too late that background checks are an imperative part of the rental process that will ultimately save you grief down the road:

> *It seemed like my properties had some sort of curse on them. Otherwise, how could perfectly good applicants somehow self-destruct just weeks after moving in?*
>
> *I first began to wise up about this when I got not one but three separate calls from collection agencies about a tenant I'd just rented to. I kept telling the callers that they had the wrong party, since my tenant's record was clean when I checked it. Finally, one of the creditors gave me a description of the tenant and her car, and I realized that I'd somehow missed something. What I'd missed was the fact that I was being deliberately misled with wrong information.*

Since learning this lesson, Lily became an application-checking fiend, looking at driver's licenses, credit cards, and even passports. These are all good documents to review in your effort to maintain a reliable pool of renters. You can also:

- Cross-check current addresses with those on the credit report.
- Cross-check owner's names with those of landlords on the application.
- Verify phone numbers.

&- Have a firm policy that nobody gets to live in one of your houses if you find any sort of falsity on their application.

As for Lily, after she discovered that close to 60 percent of her applicants were giving wrong information, she developed a full-page instruction form explaining to all potential tenants that lying about their rental, credit, criminal, or work history would result in automatic rejection and loss of their application fee. She has since rejected eight out of the last ten applicants she's had due to falsification of the application. There's an old saying, "Let the buyer beware." It might make more sense to say, "Let the property owner beware, or the property owner will be sorry."

INTERACTING WITH POTENTIAL TENANTS

Now that you have the main principles of rental real estate investing in your brain, you can really start to hit the pavement to find and work with potential renters. And that process can be rife with challenges. Of all the ideas we've looked at so far, the one that causes property owners the most trouble is the last topic we just discussed: the process of finding good tenants for your rental property. So for the balance of this chapter we'll focus our attention on that topic. After all, if you're going to create passive income through rental properties, you're going to need people to live in those properties and pay the rent. And it can't be just anybody.

Finding and Prescreening Your Tenants

The process of finding tenants virtually always starts with placing an ad on rental property sites like Apartments.com, Zillow.com, Rent.com, or Trulia.com. Usually ads for house rentals generate quite a few calls, especially when interest rates are high and people are thinking of renting rather than buying. If your property is one that appeals to tenants beyond college age (and especially to people with children), you may find that some want to rent with an option to buy. This can be a very desirable situation, because once a family is established in a property, it may suit them to pay close to your asking price rather than dealing with the cost of another move.

In any case, your first move should be a suggestion that interested parties drive by the property to see if it's appealing. You should do this before making an appointment to actually show them the house. This policy will cut down on the time you spend standing on the porch, waiting for a prospective tenant who does not show up.

A big part of any "no show" problem is the prescreening process. Most prospective tenants will try to tell you what they think you want to hear, especially over the telephone. They'll almost never say they can't afford the rent or that they don't understand leasing with an option to buy. Often, they'll go ahead and make an appointment that they have no intention of keeping. So you should definitely invite them to drive past the house, then call you back if they're interested. Tell them what the rent is going to be and how much you expect up front as a deposit, then invite them to make the drive by. More often than not, that's the last you'll hear from them, but at least you won't be waiting out in front of your rental house.

Review Financial Information

If and when you do meet with a prospective tenant, be prepared to ask some well-focused questions as you review their application and related financial documents:

- ⟡ What is your total household income before taxes?
- ⟡ Where are you living now, and what are you paying?
- ⟡ How long have you been there, and why are you moving?

Any applicant who seems unqualified should just be told that's the case. Do this frankly but in a friendly way. Make it clear that this is strictly a business decision and nothing more. If you want to soften the blow a bit, you can use some detached phrasing. For example, "As an owner, I need to have a very clear cutoff point regarding income. I wouldn't want to waste your time or your deposit on this rental, but can I keep your name and call you if I hear about anything else." If prospects insist on seeing the house anyway, it's a good idea to show it to them. Just make it clear that the bulk of your time has to be given to qualified renters. If you're concerned about asking questions about people's income and motives, you'll need to get over it. The ones who get offended are the last people you want to make an appointment with anyway.

Stay Within the Law

As you ask your questions, always be aware of fair housing laws and stay within the rules. Fair housing laws state that your willingness to rent or sell housing to a particular person cannot be based in any part on that person's race, religion, color, sex, handicap, nationality, or familial status. Unfortunately, there are applicants who threaten to file discrimination suits even against owners who choose not to rent to them for very legitimate reasons. But the fact that someone threatens you with a complaint should not intimidate you, provided you have followed the letter of the law.

The key to staying safe is to have clear guidelines for renting to an applicant. These guidelines should be objective, easy to quantify, and unrelated to the applicant's membership or nonmembership in a protected class. They should be nothing more and nothing less than predictors of the tenant's ability to fulfill the lease—that is, to pay the rent on time every month and keep the property in good condition.

Examples of these guidelines include the tenant's earning history, whether the tenant has ever been evicted, and how many places of residence the applicant has had in the last several years. Be sure to verify all this information.

It's a good idea to print these questions out as a form and actually fill out the form for each prospect. This avoids the appearance that you are trying to dissuade some tenants and not others. All rejected applications should be kept on file for at least three years, with a note on your reasons for rejecting the applicant. Before you begin showing your first property, call your local fair housing agency for additional advice.

If a prospect mentions leasing with an option to buy, ask whether they've ever entered into this kind of agreement before. If the answer is no, you can explain how a lease/option works, then end with, "Well, I'm not sure I explained that very well. I can give you some printed information about this after we look at the house." Then you can give them downloaded printouts at the end of the appointment. In this way, you're not to blame if they didn't understand—and they almost certainly won't understand. You're also saving time by giving them something to read rather than going through it all again during the meeting. The printouts can be accompanied by a rental application form that they can return at the next meeting.

Follow Up and Secure That Appointment

Sometimes prospects take an application and never return it. They seem excited about the property when they leave and promise to get the completed application back to you in a day or two, but then you never hear from them. If the applicant seemed really attractive to you, you may be thinking about making a follow-up call—but you may also think that if applicants are really worthwhile, they would keep in touch with you.

There's actually a simple answer to this problem. Yes, you should indeed be doing follow-up calls not only to the people who took applications, but even to the people who didn't. This is the best way to get feedback as to what prospects like and dislike about your property. You can speculate all day as to why people aren't returning the applications, but the only ones who can really tell you why are the people themselves. By the way, there's an obvious means of avoiding this problem in the first place. Ask people to fill out the application on site rather than return it to you. In your initial phone call, you can ask applicants to bring a driver's license or photo ID and a $20 application fee in the form of a certified check, money order, or cash. This way, they can actually apply before they have second thoughts or find another property.

Instead of winging it with each prospect to schedule an appointment, set aside a period of time each week that seems convenient for most people. Saturday from 11 A.M. to 1 P.M. usually works well. You should also be flexible, however, and if they really can't make the scheduled time, you can offer alternatives. Just remember that being customer friendly is always a good idea, but building your personal schedule around potential tenants is always a bad idea. You can appear to be accommodating them without inconveniencing yourself by offering several appointment times. The truth is, tenants won't appreciate you any more because you jump when they say to jump. In fact, it sets a tone for the rest of your relationship that you probably don't want to encourage.

Some owners ask prospects to call an hour before the appointment to confirm. Use your own judgment about whether to do this. You don't want to be treating potential tenants like children, but you also want to maximize the chances that they'll actually show up. A good trick is to say that you always forget appointments, so the call is really for your benefit.

HAVE A PLAN FOR PROPERTY MANAGEMENT

How much or little hands-on property management you do is entirely up to you and depends on how much you are (or are not) willing to pay someone to do it for you. You might enjoy the day-to-day realities of managing property, but remember, your goal is to have a passive income stream. However, no matter what you decide, there will be some management involved. Let's talk about some basic tips to get you in the property management mindset.

If you're a landlord or just looking to make money with real estate, it's crucial to understand how to manage a property the right way. It's not just about knowing how to fix things when they break. As a property manager, especially as a first-time landlord, you'll be forced to wear many hats. How you manage that property is going to either make or break your chances for success.

What's not so obvious or straightforward is how you go about managing the property. If you don't have the time or you do not live in the same town as your rental properties, no problem. Find a good, local property manager that can take care of all the details for you, and make sure they are well-versed in the type of property you are renting, whether that is primary residences for long-term renters or vacation rentals. If you have the time, and you're just starting, then you likely want to save the hefty fee that often comes with property management companies that take the reins. But you better be prepared to put in the time, because you won't find this easy to do.

While there are likely hundreds of property management tips for running a tight ship, the following tips are going to help you elevate your skill set. The goal? Expertly manage the entire experience. We're not just talking about finding the right tenants and charging the right price. You want to create a healthy and vibrant environment where you're not squeezing every last penny out of your short-term guests (think the growing Airbnb market) or long-term tenants, and where everything in the home works and isn't on the verge of failure or disrepair.

How you go about doing that will either set you apart in a good way or a bad way. Michael Joseph and Tom Feldhusen, co-founders of InvitedHome, have some advice about the world of property management. They built a small empire on true foundational values, leveraging the currency of trust while systemizing and digitizing crucial procedures over the course of a decade of growth.

They say that managing property the right way is all about transparency, hard work, and communication. At the end of the day, you have to set the right expectations by going the extra mile and ensuring that you have clear lines of communications open. One of the ways you can find yourself getting into hot water is if you set the wrong expectations and you fail to communicate.

For example, when it comes to short-term rentals, such as an Airbnb property, if you describe a feature that's not available in the home, it's not the end of the world. But if you fail to communicate that mistake with the guest and you allow the problem to fester, you could have a major issue on your hands that will likely result in a complaint. The stakes may be even higher if you do that with a long-term property. For example, if you advertise that you will cover the cost of utilities, then opt out of doing so after a long-term lease is signed, you may be in breach of your rental contract. Communication here is the key. Every dispute can be resolved with the proper amount of communication and determination of the problem that needs to be solved.

If you're looking to do this the right way, you can go it alone, or you can scour the area for an expert property manager who can help take some of the pressure off. Joseph and Felduhsen say that depending on the management level you're seeking, you're looking at rates of roughly 10 to 30 percent and up of the gross rental fees. For short-term vacation rentals, there's still a significant upside even with a property management team helping you out. Check out these tips for getting your property management right.

Get to Know Your Home

When you purchase a new property, your first step should be to get to know the home and all its systems. Each of your home's systems have a specific service interval and lifespan. The last thing you want to happen when you're renting out your home is for one of these systems to fail and have the cause be due to the lack of preventative maintenance or care.

Services like Home Manager and Breezeway enable home owners and property managers to track home systems and take care of preventative maintenance. Leading property management companies have their own proprietary systems, like InvitedHome's HomeCraft™ technology.

Plan to Reinvest in Your Home

Plan to reinvest in it with part of the revenue you earn from the home during the year. This will keep your home in tip-top shape.

Create a Financial Plan

Understand how much your home will likely generate in long- or short-term rental revenues, which is dependent on three key factors:

1. Its specific location
2. Level of luxury
3. Its size and amenities

Professional vacation rental management companies use data to accurately predict the revenue of a home. Without access to that data, you'll have to do your due diligence and scour sites online and research rates. However, advertised rental rates aren't always a prediction of the revenue you can expect to receive, and you'll be far removed from knowledge pertaining to occupancy rates.

Work with a Knowledgeable Real Estate Agent

A realtor's knowledge of the rental business, especially in the vacation market, is often varied. Some have great firsthand insight into the industry. Others know little to nothing about it. And, while they might be able to offer property management tips, whatever their expertise might be, it's important that you work with agents who understand the business, especially in the early stages of finding, buying, and managing homes that are intended to be used as vacation or long-term rentals.

Vet Several Property Managers

Before you hire a property manager, be sure you interview multiple companies. Do they have a local presence? What type of reputation do they have? Do they rank high on search engines like Google for searches relevant to your area? Find out how the property management company approaches these three key areas for managing your home:

- Maximizing your revenue generated from the home
- Caring for your home and ensuring a great experience for you when you come to town
- Providing for transparent and honest communications

Provide Easy-to-Use Instructions

When guests rent a home, they don't want to spend all their time figuring out how to use that home. Make it simple for them. How do you use the appliances, the hot water heater, the furnace, and A/C? How about any music systems or the laundry, if you plan to offer those? Great property management companies will go through and detail all of this for you so that you won't have to do it yourself. But if you do it on your own, be extremely thorough and meticulous.

Ensure Proper Levels of Inventory for Vacation Rentals

If you choose to make your rental vacation-oriented for the Airbnb crowd, you will want to make sure you have plenty of inventory available. One of the biggest reasons why guests rent homes and travel in groups is so they can cook and eat their meals together. Some of the best memories are created around the dining experience. So don't hamper it by lacking kitchen essentials. Properly stock the kitchen and other home essentials to ensure that nothing is lacking. If you're unsure, find a great property management company to help you identify what's missing.

Think of Your Home Like a Hospitality Business

If you're running your home as a rental, treat it like a hospitality business. The care and attention that most fine hotels put into their facilities and rooms is second to none. While a property management company can help you with this, if you're going it alone, you need a genuine desire to please your renters. If it feels more like a nuisance to you, then you shouldn't manage the guests because your reviews will ultimately reflect the negative experience received.

Be Realistic about Your Pricing

One of the biggest mistakes homeowners and sometimes even property managers make is setting the rental price too high. Be realistic about your approach here. Do the research. Check what others are charging, and do not overprice your home. Finding that sweet spot might be hard, but that's the trick if you want to have high occupancy rates. This is one of the property management tips that could make or break your year when it comes to financial growth.

Build a Good Relationship with Your Housekeeping Team

Whether you choose to employ a cleaning company to tidy up between guests (if you are running a vacation rental) or between long-term tenants, having a good housekeeping team is crucial. If you're doing your own property management, you should put a high level of care and attention into finding and interviewing the right team. If they're careless and they overlook the details, it's going to reflect on you. You'll receive complaints and negative reviews, and your business will suffer. If you do find a great team, set the expectations clearly in writing at the beginning of the relationship to help avoid conflict in the future.

Have a Solid Marketing Plan

Simply listing your vacation home on Airbnb or your long-term rental on Apartments.com isn't a marketing plan. It's a start. But it's not a plan. Today, there are many channels in which you can market your home as a rental, but the flood of inventory has made the competition fierce. If your goal is to maximize your revenue, do research on how to optimize your listing and consider using software like MyVR.com to keep everything up to date on all the listing sites.

Take Preventative Maintenance Seriously

Create a preventative maintenance plan for your home and stick to it. This is a cornerstone of good property management. You don't want a boiler to bust during a winter with subzero temperatures, resulting in irate tenants. Ninety-five percent of these issues are preventable with the proper maintenance of your home. Not only will you avoid paying double overtime for repairs, but you'll also avoid having to refund all or part of a short-term guest's rental fee or long-term tenant's rent. Take this seriously.

Dynamic Pricing and Revenue Management

Airlines and hotels have used a dynamic pricing and revenue management model for years. The underlying concept? Ensure that pricing adjusts with demand and supply. If you're managing your home, learn everything there is to know about revenue management with tools like HomeAway's MarketMaker™ or Beyond Pricing to help you price your home appropriately and vary that pricing based on the market.

PARTING THOUGHTS

The practices we've discussed in our two chapters on real estate investment are followed by virtually all successful property owners. There's also one other quality that's shared by all high-performing real estate investors, and that's a personal code of ethics. Although the real estate business seems to be about roofing and siding and money, it's actually about human beings finding places to live. Your decisions will affect many people in very basic ways. As a result, it's important to decide how you'll act with tenants, applicants, service providers, and everyone else you'll meet in the course of your work. Meeting the highest ethical standards is not difficult. Just ask yourself, "Am I behaving fairly?" and, "Is this the way I would like to be treated if I were a renter instead of an owner?" When you are able to answer both these questions in the affirmative, your real estate business will soon be almost running itself. Your reputation as a fair-minded owner will grow, and so will your passive income stream.

CHAPTER NINE

BUILDING WEALTH WITH A SIDE HUSTLE

If you read the biographies of people who have been successful in business over the past hundred years, you'll find that none of them get there by being overly cautious—or even by being cautious at all. They saw a clear connection between big risk and big reward, and they were eager to take the big risks. But here's the problem. There are lots of biographies of successful people, but there aren't nearly as many of people who were unsuccessful. And you know what? Unsuccessful people are also drawn to big risks. It's just that they're going to stay unsuccessful until the risks pay off—and for many people, that day never comes.

For your purposes, the ultimate success story is the power to support yourself entirely by passive income. That means you have a sufficient number of income streams (or one big one) so that you don't need money from any other source. In this chapter, you're going to see how you can move closer toward that goal by cultivating skills you already have in place through your "day job." In other words, we are going to talk about some moves you can make to take your side hustle passive. We're also going to see that it really is a process of moving toward the goal over a period of time and not just arriving there all of a sudden. But it can be done. In fact, more and more people are finding that it has to be done because the alternatives are rapidly fading away.

PLAN YOUR SIDE HUSTLE

Since the middle of the 20th century, America was built on the concept of long-term employment with one company. It began during the 1940s, when workers were desperately needed for the war effort. The whole idea of firing people began to evaporate. Losing a job had been such a potent threat during the early part of the century, when men like Andrew Carnegie and Henry Ford tried to break strikes by closing plants and firing workers. But when every pair of hands was desperately needed, companies began to provide cradle-to-grave security, including health benefits, vacations, and elaborate grievance procedures.

That was then, and this is now. Today almost nobody stays with one company for a whole career and increasing numbers of people are never with a company at all—even more people are taking the skills they gain during the 9-to-5 hours and converting them into paying gigs on the side that convert into viable passive income streams. Being an entrepreneur is becoming the norm, not the exception. Lots of positives have come with this profound change—but not many people would say that it happens by itself. It takes lots of planning and it also takes lots of guts. Check out Adriana's story and see if you can recognize yourself in her side hustle experience:

I graduated from college four years ago with a degree in graphic design. Lots of my friends who had the same degree were talking about starting their own businesses. It seemed very simple: Work at home, build up a network of referrals, and then create intellectual property that I can license out. Pretty soon all you'll need to do is cash the checks. But except for myself, not one person has made it work— and for a long time I had to do a lot more than just cash checks. That's why most people work for someone else, even if they know that trading time for money is a losing game. And to be honest, I couldn't have been a freelancer and developed passive income streams if I didn't have a financial cushion in place first.

When I decided to stop trading my time for money, I saw that my goal in life was to do the exact opposite. I wanted to have enough money in exchange for the smallest possible amount of time. As I thought it over, it seemed like there were three practical ways of reaching that goal.

First, I could become a full-time independent contractor—a classic freelancer. At first, this seemed like the easiest route. I would have flexible hours, the ability to pursue any job or assignment that appealed to me, and the flexibility to change my tactics and strategies at a moment's notice. The downside was having to charge low fees at the start, because I didn't have experience. And at least at the outset, I would still be trading money for time until I had the capital to build passive income streams.

It also occurred to me that I could actually start an organization—a company with an office and some employees and, of course, myself as the head. That would mean getting investors or a bank loan—but I also felt it would give me more credibility than if I was just sitting at home with my computer and my telephone. This route began to seem more attractive when a major client at my current job took me aside for a confidential chat. I was flattered when he told me that he was happy working with my employer, but he was especially impressed with my work individually. He even suggested that if I were to start my own operation, he would probably follow me with his account.

That was very exciting, but I could also see a potential complication. What if this client turned out to be less than pleased with my work once I no longer had the support and infrastructure of my current employer? I had better be prepared for a lot of hard work—and in a sense, my client would actually be my new boss. Officially, I would be self-employed, but the reality would be something very different.

Finally, I decided that a third route was best. I put off leaving my job for a while, but I also started pursuing passive income ideas in the meantime. With this route, I had enough money to pay my bills and still enter the arena of entrepreneurship. The only trouble was, I could be wasting valuable time. As long as I was still working 9 to 5, I couldn't develop my ideas to the maximum. Also, as long as I was still getting a paycheck I was going to need a lot of discipline. I would be tempted to just pay my bills and goof off the rest of the time.

In the end, I did go with the third option—but about three months ago I found myself gravitating toward the life of a full-time entrepreneur. I've found that it really is very difficult to be a successful risk taker when you're also working all day to keep a safety net in place. Also, I did have some money saved so that I wouldn't have to worry about paying bills for at least six months, provided I didn't go on any shopping sprees. So, I took the plunge. And here's the main thing I've learned: There are lots of opportunities when you're working for yourself, and there are many ways to create passive income streams. There may even be too many ways—because what really makes the difference is being able to turn down good opportunities so you can pursue better ones. You need to think long and hard about your core plan, and don't let a little cash change your mind.

Sound familiar? Adriana's experience is a common one: She wanted that financial peace that passive income can bring, but she still needed a safety net first. And that's OK. No one (at least, not many people) can just walk out of a job on a whim and strike out on their own without first laying some groundwork by pursuing a side hustle or experimenting with passive income ideas. So, make the right moves as you transition out of your day job. If you're looking for financial independence and creative ways to bring that about, there are some key ideas to keep in mind.

Start by Saving

First, start saving some money before you stop being a salaried worker. In other words, don't quit your day job—at least not right away. Today there is no such thing as job security, but when you're an entrepreneur the risk is all on you. So you'd better have some savings. It's a good idea to have about six months of living expenses on hand. You should be especially careful about health insurance. This is a big expense—often it's equal to what people pay in rent. But you really need to get it when you can. If you have a health problem without having insurance, not only will you have trouble funding treatment, but getting insurance later will be even more difficult.

Build a Client List

Next, have some clients already on board when you go out on your own. You should be doing freelance work on the side long before you switch to it full time. If you don't, it can take months or even years to establish accounts that will pay you at a decent rate. So in the time leading up to the switch, make sure you have clients lined up well before you quit. Then crunch some numbers. It will be exciting to be out on your own supporting yourself with multiple income streams— but if you happen to be married with a family, you had better know exactly what your expenses are and whether you'll be able to meet them every month. When you consider those expenses, be sure to add in the cost of health insurance and any retirement plan you're funding. Working on your own takes planning and financial discipline, so make sure you're ready for it.

The truth is, even if you're no longer on salary, you still have "employers," except now they're called clients or customers. You have deadlines and commitments, and unlike many people in the corporate world, if you don't meet your deadlines, you don't get paid. So you no longer have a boss looking over your shoulder and you're no longer just trading time for money, but the trade-off is that you have to manage yourself carefully. You have to "be your own boss" in a very literal sense.

Master Time Management

Here's a third point. Effective time management should become a major priority. One system that works well involves dividing the day into three parts. Start the morning by catching up on any projects in which you may have fallen behind during the previous day. Sometimes, no matter how well you've planned, things will come up that prevent you from getting work done as you'd intended. So, don't do anything the following day until you've caught up. Sometimes you may not have to do this at all, and other times it may take most of the morning. In any case, use the middle of the day for staying on track with your various responsibilities. If you have a website business, make sure you update it. If you have stock market or real estate investments, stay on top of them. Finally, use the afternoon to look for new opportunities and to stay in touch with people who can help you find them. When you're first setting up your passive income streams, there will be days when you're working harder than ever. But if you do it right, those will only be days—not years. Keep your eye on the prize, and the prize will come.

MAKE TIME FOR MAINTENANCE AND GROWTH PROJECTS

One of the best things about having a schedule is that you can break it if you need to—but at least you'll be aware of what you're doing. When circumstances change, priorities have to change, too, at least in the short term. Agility and flexibility are a couple of big advantages that entrepreneurs have over larger organizations. Many opportunities come up that are time sensitive, and if you're locked into an artificially rigid schedule, you'll miss them. The trick is to know the difference between maintenance work and a chance for real growth work. You need both, and you've got to make time for both.

What do we mean by maintenance work vs. growth work? Well, some work actively generates passive income for you, while some work has to be done to keep your income stream coming in. There's actually no such thing as purely passive income. At the very least, you have to collect your checks and deposit them, right? And there's usually a lot more than that. Rental property has to be managed. Websites have to be kept up-to-date. Maintenance work has to be done on a regular basis—daily, weekly, or monthly—and there are consequences if you don't get it done. Growth work, on the other hand, doesn't have a consequence attached to it unless you give it one. So, make sure you know how much maintenance work your income streams require so you know how much time you really have for growth projects. Examples of growth projects include:

- Webinars
- Courses
- Ebooks
- Marketing assets
- Paid newsletters
- Projects for new clients
- Content

You'll find it best to work on only one growth project at a time. Keep working on it until it starts working for you. When a project is first starting out, do whatever it takes to get it to the point that it has a life of its own. That may mean getting it to the point where you can share it with potential collaborators or customers, or it may mean getting it to the point that it can start to generate income. Once a project has started earning passive revenue, let it work for you while you work on something else.

THE PERFECT SIDE HUSTLE: INTELLECTUAL PROPERTY

Sometimes people assume that leaving the salaried world means starting a whole new life. In a way that's true, but it shouldn't mean abandoning everything you've learned and gotten good at. If you're working in the marketing department of a large corporation, for

TAKE YOUR SIDE HUSTLE TO THE NEXT LEVEL

Few people are lucky enough love their 9-to-5s, and more and more people are finding themselves doing something else on the side, either to add to their income or to feed their passion. Sometimes, those side hustles start to feel more and more like the real thing, and suddenly, these people are dreaming about running a business of their own. Sound familiar? If you're one of the thousands of people dreaming about turning your side hustle into a true business, you're not alone.

Moving away from a steady, full-time position to being on your own is the scariest, yet most invigorating feeling in the world. Most people consider entrepreneurship either unattainable or, honestly, highly romanticized. The reality is that neither is correct. Being an entrepreneur is a *ton* of work, but it's also completely possible. Here are five tips to follow if you want to go pro:

1. *Be clear and honest with yourself about when it's time to make the jump.* Giving up the benefits and security that come with a full-time job is scary, and sometimes unrealistic, but it's also dangerous to keep waiting until the time feels right. Ask yourself exactly what you need to have before you can make your side gig your new reality. A good rule of thumb is to have enough savings to live for about six months without income, and/or with the income you already have from your side clients. You should also have a clear idea of who your potential clients may be and how to connect with them.

   After taking care of the logistical considerations, try to avoid dragging your feet. According to the British Psychological Society, you're 91 percent more likely to

SIDE HUSTLE, CONTINUED

accomplish something if you give yourself a deadline. So do it! Hold yourself accountable. Maybe you're not willing to stay at your current job beyond a certain date, or maybe there will be other indicators that will make you certain that it's time to go. If your current role isn't fulfilling and the passion is gone, it may be the perfect catalyst for making the jump.

2. *Before you quit, put the processes in place to help your side gig scale.* Early on, business organization and strategizing is a huge component of success. You'll need to limit stress and create as much efficiency and ease as possible in your daily systems. This could mean scheduling things carefully or using free software to make your work more effective. Try as best you can to not switch back and forth between your different focus areas within the same day. Going back and forth between tasks that are not related is inefficient and breaks focus. Give your brain a break and keep yourself on one straight road each day.

Digitizing your work can help, too. According to Accenture, companies that use cloud collaboration tools with their teams improve productivity, have greater clarity about what's going on in their business, and save money. When you start out, it can feel silly to keep documents in a shareable cloud space (like Google Drive, Dropbox, or whatever option you like best), but you need to have the structures in place so that you're organized and ready for the time if/when you hire a team to support you. This is a good thing to play around with *before* you quit your main gig. Having the tools and processes you know work well for you ready to go when you make the switch can make ramp-up time easier.

SIDE HUSTLE, CONTINUED

3. *Work hard and be humble.* Your time is valuable, but as a new entrepreneur you can't treat it like currency. Be prepared to put in lots of hours with minimal return at first. Initially, time may not correlate with financial success; this is an incredibly important mindset to remember. Your time isn't money, yet. It's groundwork. Building a side gig up from the ground up requires wearing a lot of different hats. If you want your business to succeed, you have to be ready to play customer service rep, salesperson, individual contributor, and HR.

    If you're feeling overwhelmed, break the work down further. Spend more time working on the day-to-day tasks and checking things off the to-do list. These are all working toward your big vision, but in small doable pieces rather than hefty overwhelming ones. Try not to consider any task beneath you and take some time to truly understand what goes into each part of your business. You won't have a boss telling you what's right or wrong, so you'll need to build a sense of self-accountability—one of the toughest parts of being an entrepreneur. Take notes about the challenges you face in each aspect of your business so you'll know what anyone you might hire will have to cope with. It's your best chance to uncover important considerations and think about down the line what resources might need to go where.

4. *Surround yourself with smart people—even if you never plan to work with them.* As much as entrepreneurship can be a solitary job, especially in the beginning, it's vital to your success to remember how others can help you thrive. Invest your time in like-minded people. Take time to get to know others and their stories and create valuable relationships. So much of success

SIDE HUSTLE, CONTINUED

is built from opportunities or inspiration from people we know. Find people you connect with to talk about your ideas, write about your ideas online, and build a community that empowers you. Take advantage of those around you who want to see you succeed. You'll be surprised at how much people want to help! The number of new startups and small businesses has dropped dramatically in recent years, nearing a 40-year low in 2016. The landscape has gotten tougher, which makes being an entrepreneur scarier. Turning a side hustle into the real thing is not easy. But, just as with most other big decisions in life, there are always lessons to be learned no matter what happens. Be thoughtful, take smart risks, and see where your side hustle can go.

instance, you don't have to go into an entirely new field just because you want to become self-supporting. Instead, ask yourself how you can create passive income by using the skills you've already developed.

When you do this, you'll find that often it takes you into the area of intellectual property—that is, work you've generated in the form of words, sounds, or images. All these can be copyrighted, and you can gain income by allowing access to them. In short, intellectual property is the ultimate side hustle.

Here's an example. Marli, a freelance translator, noticed a discussion on the internet about copyright issues. She wondered, "Do I have any rights to the translations I produce?" The answer turned out to be yes, especially if there was no contract stating otherwise. This led to some very productive ideas for creating passive income. Here is her story:

When a piece of writing has been out of print for many years, the copyright ownership of that book may lapse. Or in the case of a foreign language document, it may be the copyright of the translation that loses force. As a translator, the difference between these two issues is very important to me. For example, no one owns the copyright to Shakespeare's plays. I can print an edition of the plays on my computer and try to sell it, and neither Shakespeare's heirs not his many publishers can object. But if I translate Hamlet *into Finnish, and someone in Finland wants to publish my translation, they have to get my permission—even though the play itself is in the public domain.*

This has opened a huge resource for me in producing passive income. In the past, I had taken it for granted that any translation work I did became the property of the client who paid me, as part of a work-for-hire deal. But that's true unless I agree to it, so retaining rights to my translations can become a negotiating point for me. And if I translate something on my own rather than as part of a work-for-hire deal, I own the rights to the finished work even if the original was in the public domain. That means I'm entitled to a royalty check whenever anyone wants to use my translation. Once I understood this, I immediately started translating some well-known public domain stories, especially stories that are often anthologized. This has been an excellent passive income stream for me—and the more stories I translate, the bigger it gets.

As technology continues to advance, you may be surprised by what intellectual property has come to include. For example, English may be your only language, but you can still own the rights to a translation. Even if you used a computer-aided translation program to complete the work, the rights to the translated text still belong to you. So be aware of the many areas of your life in which you may be producing something that qualifies as intellectual property. If you're in service industries such as consulting, photography, or even manufacturing, there's a good chance this is the case—and if it is, here are some steps you should take right away.

Copyright It

Assert your rights by inserting a copyright notice, getting trade or service marks, or obtaining patents to protect the product of your work. You must protect the fruits of your labors by making it difficult for others to sell it or use it for their own profit. It's actually much easier than you might think to copyright something. Usually just stating that material is copyrighted—at the bottom of a website, for example—is legally all it takes. With printed texts, just draw the letter "c" with a circle around it, then write your name. Copywriting designs or software innovations can be a bit more complicated, so it's a good idea to consult an attorney. But don't neglect taking this step. You can't draw passive income on intellectual property unless you can prove that the property is yours.

Charge a Protected License Fee

Charge a separate fee for your protected materials whenever they are used. This can provide a major passive income stream. And if you can't be sure that you'll be able to control the use of your creations, you can deal with that problem in your original contract.

Here's a case in point. You're a landscape architect and you create a beautiful design for the parklike area around a new office complex. You invested talent and imagination in the creation of this design. You also needed a lot of time to produce it—not just the hours you spent making the design itself, but also the years of experience that you needed beforehand. Even more important, the design you've produced will now be available to anyone who visits the office park. If another real estate developer wants to develop a similar office park, it's very possible that the developer will copy your design without any compensation for you. To deal with that possibility, you can negotiate a licensing fee from your original client in addition to whatever your one-time payment might be. This will insure you against the probability that your efforts will be reused for profit by others.

If your client won't agree to the licensing fee, then you have a strong argument for drastically increasing your basic fee. If you're creating intellectual property, you're an artist in your own right—and in the art world, there's a good reason why prices can be sky-high. Let's say that a painter creates a landscape and it sells for $10,000.

As the painter continues their career and builds a reputation, the value of the landscape begins to increase—so that when the original owner puts it on the market, it sells for a $100,000. That's a profit of $90,000 for the owner, of which the artist gets not one cent. Therefore, the artist is fully justified in building a fee for the owner's future profit into the artist's original price. Although it's possible in the world of fine art, you can offer your clients the option of a continuing licensing fee and the passive income it will bring. Or you can up your original price. Since licensing is the best option for both parties, chances are they'll go for it—and you'll be getting checks for years to come.

Negotiate a Royalty

You can also negotiate a royalty if a client uses your copyrighted material to generate sales. This is a legitimate fee for the continuing use of your intellectual property by a profit-making enterprise. What's more, when this royalty or licensing fee is taxed as passive income, it can be offset by passive losses generated by other sideline activities, such as real estate investing, for example. Unless you are a real estate professional—that is, you spend at least 50 percent of your time in the real estate business—your passive losses in real estate can be deducted from other earned passive income up to a legal limit. You'll want to check with a tax accountant for the details.

Subcontract Work

As you become more successful and better known, you can create passive income by subcontracting work to other professionals. You can outsource portions of the work necessary to create the intellectual property you sell, from content management to creation. If you do choose to hire someone to create an element of intellectual property you sell, be sure to have both parties sign off on an agreement that allows you to either license or purchase their work outright for inclusion in your content. For example, if you want to create an online course module, but are terrible at design, outsource that function and create an agreement that gives you ownership of the design. Outsourcing some of these functions can vastly increase the total volume of work you can handle, and the income you make will be compensation for your administration and quality control efforts.

Market Your Intellectual Property

There are plenty of opportunities out there to grow your side hustle by way of intellectual property once you start thinking creatively. In fact, after you take advantage of all the possibilities in your primary area of primary area of expertise, you can begin looking in other related areas for both additional passive income and a way to market what you already sell.

An excellent way to start is by joining an affiliate program related to your main area of expertise. You already read about these programs in Chapter 4, but to reiterate, these programs allow you to collect a commission for any sales that come through those links. By associating your own intellectual property with related affiliate programs, you not only bank extra cash, but you also get the halo effect of being linked to other companies.

Aside from the obvious suggestion of creating a landing page for your side hustle, you should also incorporate a social media marketing push with it. Most social media sites now allow for direct selling right on their platforms, which helps get your message out to your social network and create an impactful sales funnel.

───────── **PARTING THOUGHTS** ─────────

In this chapter, we've seen how the workplace is becoming a much more improvisational, entrepreneurial setting. We've seen also how you can profit from that. The first step is making a commitment to stop trading money for time—but you also need sufficient funds to act on that commitment until some money starts coming in. We've also seen how the concept of intellectual property can open up income streams you may never have imagined. To access those streams, you just need a certain amount of creativity—plus the assertiveness to get paid for what you've created. It can definitely be done. Just remember, as we said at the start of this chapter, it won't happen by itself.

CHAPTER TEN

GOING SOLO WITH MULTILEVEL MARKETING

You have explored several passive income options so far. But there's one that you might be overlooking because you've talked yourself out it—multilevel marketing, or direct sales. Now, before you turn your nose up and think we're suggesting you host house parties selling products no one needs, rest assured that multilevel marketing (also known as MLM) is experiencing a renaissance of sorts. This type of passive income stream has long been surrounded by a certain amount of controversy. For some, it's a direct path to passive income. For others, it's a cautionary tale about being your own best customer. But if done right, MLM can be a profitable passive income stream.

Whether we admit it or not, Americans have always had mixed feelings about the benefits of hard work. On the one hand, we admire people who live by the sweat of their brow—and we really admire people who get ahead that way. At the same time, we don't really hold a grudge against those who inherit wealth, especially if they share some of it through philanthropic or charitable causes. In other parts of the world there's a deep resentment against the rich, but that anger has never really taken hold in this country—probably because so many of us want to be rich ourselves. And given a choice, most of us would like to get rich the easy way rather than the hard way. We'd prefer to win the lottery tomorrow to spending 20 or 30 years building up a business. And we'd rather just get a check in the mail or a wire deposit to our bank account than work 9 to 5 all week for a payment on Friday. In short, we admire people who work really hard, but in our own lives we'd like to replace that hard work with passive income to the greatest possible extent.

These dual feelings about work and wealth and what it all means come into sharp focus around the topic of MLM. In a sense, multilevel marketing is the ultimate in passive income. In multilevel marketing, if things go according to plan, you quickly develop an ever-expanding group of subordinates whose work benefits you as well as them. To see how that happens—or how it's supposed to happen—let's start with the basics.

MLM 101

Multilevel marketing—also called MLM, or network marketing—is a way of selling products and services through a chain of semi-independent distributors rather than traditional retail outlets, such as stores or mail order. Each MLM distributor has two basic jobs. The first job is to sell the company's products or services, and the second job is to recruit more distributors for the same purpose.

In turn, each new recruit a distributor brings into the organization is encouraged to bring in his or her own recruits. Eventually, an active distributor develops a substructure known as a downline. Once that's happened, the distributor not only gets commissions on his or her own direct sales, but also gets a commission on the sales of the distributors in the downline. There are also usually performance bonuses for reaching certain sales levels. Since each distributor profits from sales of the downline, it is to the advantage of the distributor to help those below them to succeed.

The basic concept of MLM has existed for at least a century, but in post-war America, its first big success was the company then known as Amway—a contraction of "American Way"—which was founded in 1959. Since then, Amway has conducted business through a number of affiliated companies in more than 90 countries and territories around the world, as well as the United States and Canada. This family of companies reported sales of $8.6 billion in 2017. Its product lines include personal care products, jewelry, dietary supplements, water purifiers, air purifiers, insurance, various home goods, and cosmetics. As the Amway website puts it, "For more than 45 years, Amway Corporation has enabled people to have a business of their own."

Other direct selling business models followed suit over the years, including many you've likely heard of:

- Herbalife
- Longaberger
- The Pampered Chef
- Mary Kay
- Avon
- Arbonne
- Juice Plus
- LuLaRoe
- Medifast
- Rodan + Fields
- Scentsy
- PartyLite

And this is just a sampling of the MLM companies in the sales world. Hundreds more exist, all with a varying degree of success for those who participate in their programs. What this list proves is that MLM has come a long way since Amway started the direct selling revolution—and it's not going away anytime soon. Yet despite the longevity of this passive income model, MLM does have its detractors.

THE MLM CONTROVERSY

It has sometimes been asserted that MLM is not a pyramid scheme because actual physical products are sold and change hands. But the sale of products by itself is not a defense against unfair trade practices set forth in federal and state law. MLM is a legal form of business only if it conforms to rigid conditions set forth by the Federal Trade Commission (FTC) and by state regulations. Many MLMs ignore these guidelines and operate only because they have not been prosecuted. Moreover, recent court rulings are using a 70 percent rule (initiated in 1979 after questions about Amway's legal standing were brought to light) to determine an MLM's legality. That means that at least 70 percent of all goods sold by an MLM company must be sold at a wholesale or retail price.

This ruling has been widely interpreted among the MLM community ever since. Does it mean that 70 percent of the product must be sold to nondistributors only? Or can it be purchased by those doing the selling (even though the rule was established to prevent distributor hoarding just to make commission for the month)? It's a somewhat confusing rule, so your best bet to make sure you're within the law is to check with the FTC for current rulings and regulations. For the most up-to-date information on the FTC's stance on the industry, you can visit www.ftc.gov/tips-advice/business-center/guidance/business-guidance-concerning-multi-level-marketing.

The 1979 Amway ruling and many other decisions that followed addressed not only how products were purchased, but also how people were compensated. There are many reputable MLM programs, but also many that are set up as pyramid schemes. Your job, when deciding whether this is the right passive income stream for you, is to do your due diligence and research the reputation of the companies you're considering. While most multilevel marketing plans are legitimate, others are illegal pyramid schemes. Needless to say, it's very important to know the difference. In pyramids, commissions are based on the number of distributors recruited. Most of the product sales are made to these distributors for their personal use in the form of samples. They never actually reach the public at large. The various goods and services—which can be anything from vitamins to car leases—are only props to make the enterprise look legitimate.

Joining a pyramid is risky because the vast majority of participants lose money. They pay the rewards of the lucky few at the top of the chain. Most people end up with nothing to show for their money except the expensive products or marketing materials they were urged to buy.

Think of it like a chain letter. At one time or another, almost everyone has been asked to participate in a chain letter scheme, with the promise of hundreds of personal checks soon appearing in your mailbox, all made out to you. Chain letters promise a phenomenal return on a small effort. They're also illegal, for the simple reason that the payoff is impossible. But to see what this implies for multilevel marketing, we need to look a bit closer at the mechanics of how chain letters work.

The simplest form of a chain letter contains a list of people's names, usually between five and ten of them. You're supposed to send a check to the top person on the list. Then you erase that top person, sliding the second person into the top position. You add yourself in the bottom position, make copies of the letter, and mail them to your friends. The promise is that you will receive huge amounts of money when your name reaches the top of the list.

Except you won't. Chain letters can't work, and here's why. Let's assume that there are ten names on the list and that everyone on the list is honest and keeps perpetuating the chain. Within just a few generations of the letter—and long before your name has reached the top—thousands of people would have to have received copies. For you to get any money, the letter would have to go through ten generations, which requires the involvement of millions of people. If even a few chain letters actually continued through several cycles, the entire country would grind to a halt under the weight of billions of letters. Fortunately, that has never happened, and it never will.

So why do people think a structure like a chain letter can work? And is there a connection between this belief and the appeal of multilevel marketing? Regarding the first question, people are tempted by these schemes because the human mind does not have an intuitive grasp of the mathematical progression. There's also the fact that not much effort is required, and not much expense: You send out a couple $5 checks with the possibility of getting hundreds of such checks yourself. Along the same lines, there was a fad in the 1980s for so-called Pyramid Clubs, some of which cost $1,000 to join. There were also pyramid phone-calling schemes back then, and the internet has been a fertile field for similar scams today. But again, nobody makes any money—except possibly one person. That's the person who initiates the letter and whose name is at the top of the list. That's why you must be mindful of what type of MLM structure you're buying into. If it's nothing more than a pyramid, you won't see the payoff you're hoping to get.

THE POWER IS IN YOUR DOWNLINE

Once you get a feel for the kinds of legitimate MLM prospects out there, you can focus on details of how each company's downline works and start asking questions like, Do MLM companies set any limits on how extensive the downlines can become?

Actually, different MLM companies set different rules governing how many levels can exist through which distributors will be paid. Some link the number of levels to the total sales volume, or they simply impose an arbitrary cutoff point. In addition, once they've reached a certain sales volume, downline distributors are often allowed to split off from the parent distributor and operate as the head of their own chain. In any case, you can see the benefits to being one of the first people in the mix. You will be getting payments from everybody below you, at least until your most successful recruits have split off. Meanwhile, if you've continued your own recruiting efforts, you'll be

MLM GOES SOCIAL:
AN ENTREPRENEUR INTERVIEW WITH CHANTEL WATERBURY, FOUNDER OF CHLOE AND ISABEL

By Sarah Max, *Entrepreneur* contributor

The summer before her freshman year of college, Chantel Waterbury drove around Northern California selling Cutco cutlery door to door. She didn't realize it at the time, but that experience would have a lasting impact, both on her corporate career and decisions she would make when she launched her own company, Chloe and Isabel, in 2011.

Despite her enviable connections in retail—her resume includes fashion jewelry buyer at Macy's, director of accessories for Old Navy, and vice president of Haskell Jewels, overseeing Kenneth Cole jewelry design and merchandising—Waterbury opted to go the direct sales route with her own fashion jewelry brand.

The decision, she says, hinged largely on her desire to do more than just sell jewelry. "My bigger vision was to empower women by giving them an opportunity to make money and learn critical skills they can use elsewhere," says Waterbury.

Today, her New York-based company has roughly 85 corporate employees and a network of more than 5,000 merchandisers who sell Chloe and Isabel goods directly through pop-up stores and their own online stores. Whereas direct selling has tended to skew toward older sellers, 75 percent of Chloe and Isabel merchandisers are under the age of 35.

Entrepreneur chatted with Waterbury about how direct selling has evolved into social retailing.

Entrepreneur: Let's start with your stint selling Cutco cutlery. Were you good at it?

MLM GOES SOCIAL, CONTINUED

Waterbury: Over the course of three months, I sold $33,000 worth of knives and made enough to pay for my first two years of college. I sold to everyone in that county. The problem is that those knives last forever, so eventually I exhausted my channels. I tried selling vacuum filters, but it was tough, since I didn't really believe in the product. Let's just say I didn't sell those to anyone I knew.

Entrepreneur: Fast forward to a few years ago, when you started your own company. You had connections in retail but decided to go the direct sales route. Why?

Waterbury: I knew always I wanted my own company and my own brand, but I didn't know how I would do it. What I did know was that when I got to the top of the corporate ladder, something was missing. I didn't feel like I was making a big enough impact. I was really drawn to the fact that the recession was hitting Millennials the hardest. When I think of that age, I think direct sales, because that's when I did it. I didn't realize until later that direct selling isn't typically considered an opportunity for younger people.

Entrepreneur: Any other surprises?

Waterbury: Building the brand Chloe and Isabel was the easy part. The hard part was taking this old model of direct sales and revamping it for today. That's why we call it social retail. At the time, I didn't think I was creating a social platform, and I certainly didn't realize that my largest team would be in engineering. But I had a clear vision of how I wanted it to work and what tools I wanted my retailers to have.

MLM GOES SOCIAL, CONTINUED

Entrepreneur: In that respect, I'm guessing social retailing is more appealing to younger women than hosting Tupperware parties or knocking on doors.

Waterbury: When I sold directly, I was confined to a 30-mile radius. I drove to every single appointment. So definitely. What hasn't changed is the power of personal connections. If anything, they're stronger today.

Entrepreneur: Why is that?

Waterbury: Increasingly, people look to their social networks to guide their purchases. Merchandisers get so excited the first time they get an order from someone they don't know, but if they dig a little deeper, it's usually someone who knows someone they know.

Entrepreneur: How is this different from selling online via a traditional retailer?

Waterbury: Most retailers are still focusing on the sheer volume of their reviews. When you start to deal with strangers recommending something, you want power in numbers. What we're doing is much more personal because everything is ultimately being sold by someone. That said, we've noticed that people want reassurance about the products they're buying. They will come into our forum and ask other people to post a picture of something. They don't want the marketing shots. They want a real image.

Entrepreneur: Is there etiquette for selling via social channels, especially when it's your personal networks? Will there come a point when people will tune out friends selling stuff?

MLM GOES SOCIAL, CONTINUED

Waterbury: There is always etiquette! At Chloe and Isabel, we are not just a fashion brand, but a lifestyle brand. When marketing yourself, it is always about adding value to your customers, and this applies to our merchandisers as well. We encourage our community to learn a balance of marketing the jewelry, as well as marketing their personal brand, which helps to build value for their network for stronger brand affinity.

bringing more people in all the time. Every time they make a sale, you get a commission—and you also get a commission every time one of *their* recruits makes a sale. Once this gets rolling, you don't even need to make any sales of your own. It's pure passive income.

Is this too good to be true? Well, sometimes it is. For one thing, top-level distributors in MLM companies are supposed to provide training and support services for the downline. But in reality, that doesn't always happen. Sometimes new recruits are talked into joining with promises of gaining financial independence and great wealth—and that's pretty much all they're told. Out of their own pockets they have to buy samples of whatever the product might be, but there really isn't much incentive to do much selling. The real key to reaching the pot of gold is to recruit new people, so that's where the effort goes.

As with a chain letter, the cost to get started in MLM is often relatively low—sometimes less than $100 for sample products. The payoff is described as virtually unlimited, so many recruits figure, "What have I got to lose?" Yet some people are soon investing thousands of dollars in their MLM business on more sample products, meeting fees, transportation costs, promotional literature, tapes, books, and an extensive list of other materials made available for a profit by the parent company.

THE PAYOFF

So far it sounds like multilevel marketing is nothing but bad news. So let's ask another very pertinent question: Does anyone ever make money in MLM? And here's some good news. The answer is yes. But as in any other for-profit enterprise, the amount of money that can be made is proportional to the effort, time, commitment, and planning that goes into building the business. It generally takes distributors about a year of working 10 to 15 hours a week to have an income of about $1,000 a month—which isn't a bad return on investment. But the real money is in residual passive income, which can take three to five years of concentrated effort to build. Let's take a quick look at how that happens.

Each MLM will have its own compensation plan, which is simply the mechanism by which you get paid. The plans makes clear what volume of sales you need in order to get any money, as well as how many levels of downline will pay you, and under what circumstances you will qualify for bonuses. There are also hybrid plans that combine one or more elements of the basic structures. Most people are inclined to believe in whatever plan their company has in place. If they didn't believe in it, they wouldn't have signed on in the first place. Some plans are designed to pay a higher percentage of the available bonus money up front. These will be payments for personal sales and on commissions for group sales in the first three levels. Others are constructed to pay more in the deeper levels, and some spread the bonus payout across all levels of the compensation plan. Regardless of the type of plan, the key to remember is that you can make money with any of them as long as the company itself is legitimate. The product and the effort you make are what will make the difference. And that effort starts with research.

DO YOUR RESEARCH

Now that you are familiar with the basics of how MLM works, you can take that knowledge in hand as you start to vet possible companies. If you're thinking about joining a multilevel marketing plan, take time to learn about exactly what's involved. Ask some questions up front, like:

- What kind of track record does the company have?
- What products does it sell?
- What volume of products is sold to the public at large?
- Does it have the evidence to back up any claims made about the product?
- Is the product competitively priced?
- Is it likely to appeal to a large customer base?
- How much is the investment to join the plan?
- Is there a minimum monthly sales commitment to earn a commission?
- Will you be required to recruit new distributors to earn your commission?

These are just a few of the things you'll need to know. As you look more closely at the deal, more questions will occur to you—and you should not hesitate to ask them.

KNOW WHAT YOU'RE GETTING INTO

Ask questions, questions, and more questions (of the company and *yourself*) before you commit to MLM. While the potential for a strong passive revenue stream is good, you have to play your cards right to make it work for you. For example, if you think you'll get rich only by selling product, you're going to be disappointed. Remember—the power is in your downline. In addition, be aware of what the initial startup costs are so you are not surprised, and so you can determine if the investment is worth the rewards. For example, be skeptical if a distributor tells you that for the price of a startup kit you'll be on the road to riches. The startup kit usually includes some inventory and sales literature—and sometimes a commitment to sell a specific amount of the product or service each month. You may also be asked to pay for participation in training programs or for buying sales leads. You may also have to go out of pocket for the products themselves. You will have a lot of responsibilities as a distributor in addition to financial ones.

Know Your Responsibilities

Keep in mind, too, that once you are invested in MLM, you are representing the product and the company—even if you're not technically a full-time employee. If you do choose to become a distributor, be aware that you are legally responsible for claims you make about the company, its products, and the business opportunities it offers. Your responsibility applies even if you're repeating claims you read in a company brochure or advertising flier.

For example, if you solicit new distributors, you are responsible for any claims you make about the earnings potential. Be sure to describe the opportunity honestly and avoid making unrealistic promises. If those promises fall through, you could be held liable. The lesson here? Be sure to find out the company's stance on how you are expected to represent the product and brand to the public at large, customers, and potential downline partners before you commit.

In addition, be sure to verify the research behind any claims about a product's performance before repeating those claims to a potential customer. For example, if you are considering selling a medical product (like a clinical skin product), confirm the research first. You don't want to be liable for making promises your product can't keep. Use common sense when evaluating any multilevel marketing opportunity. The MLM field is growing, and solicitations to join seem to be everywhere. Its promoters would like you to believe that this is the wave of the future—a business model that's gaining momentum, growing in legitimacy, and that will eventually replace most other forms of marketing. Many people are led to believe that success will come to anyone who believes in the system and adheres to its methods. But the proof is in the research, so take the time to make sure you understand the specifics of each opportunity and the product.

Be Honest About Your Goals

Ultimately, your goal is making money. But how you get that done is up to you when it comes to MLM. You can certainly sell the product and focus your energies on building a loyal customer base. But the truth of MLM is that being a distributor with other distributors working under you is where the business model can really work for you.

That said, remember that calling something a great business model makes no more sense than calling a lottery ticket a great business venture opportunity. It's certainly true that somebody has to win the lottery, and it's also true that some investors—perhaps even thousands of them—have profited from multilevel marketing. But the retailing activity is, in fact, only a pretext for the actual core business, which is enrolling investors in an ever-expanding organization that promises exponential income growth. Be honest with yourself about your goals and your ability to sustain such a network.

In any multilevel or network marketing business, the incomes of the distributors at the top and the profits to the sponsoring corporations come from a continuous supply of new investors at the bottom. It could be argued that MLM's true constituency is not the consuming public, but the hopeful investors. The pool of these investors grows significantly in times of economic transition, globalization, and employee displacement. That's what makes MLM a strong candidate as one of your passive income streams. You should certainly do your due diligence and conduct preliminary research on the product and company, and you should also recognize the potential of MLM as a passive income stream. One way to really gauge that potential is to analyze some of the common promises you often hear from MLM companies in relation to the realities.

PROMISES VS. REALITY

Promises of quick and easy passive income and the linking of wealth to ultimate happiness are common themes in MLM recruitment marketing. That's why it is important for you to recognize when those promises are legitimate and when they are not. Here are some common promises often made by the MLM industry—and some information you should definitely have before you buy into them.

Promise 1: MLM Makes More Money

MLM promises to offer better opportunities than all other conventional business and professional models for generating large amounts of passive income.

The reality is, for *almost* everyone who invests, MLM turns out to be a losing financial proposition. Statistically, fewer than 1 percent of all MLM distributors ever earn a profit, and those earning significant passive income are an even smaller percentage. Sales and marketing obstacles account for much of this problem—but even if the business model were more feasible, sheer mathematics would limit the opportunity. The MLM business structure can support only a small number of financial winners. If a 1,000-person downline is needed to earn a substantial income, those 1,000 will need 1 million more to duplicate the success. How many people can realistically be enrolled? Much of what appears as growth is really only the continuous churning of new enrollees. The money for the rare winners comes from the constant enrollment of nonwinners. Unless there are severe limits on numbers of distributors in an area and careful evaluation of market potential, the system is also inherently unstable. Ask for financial reports and sales/downline information from any company you are considering, to make sure the earning potential is real.

Promise 2: Direct Selling Wins

You will hear that network marketing is the most popular and effective new way to bring products to market. This is because consumers like to buy products on a one-to-one basis, as the MLM model allows.

While retailing directly to friends on a one-to-one basis requires people to drastically change their buying habits, it may bridge the gap between shopping at a brick-and-mortar location and online. Yes, customers must restrict their choices, often pay more for goods, and engage in potentially awkward business relationships with close friends and relatives, but they also get personal service and the ability to test drive products without driving off-site to do so. According to the Direct Selling Association, 68 percent of consumers prefer in-person shopping to online because they can actually see, touch, and try on what they're buying.

Promise 3: MLM is the Wave of the Future

In the future, all products will be sold by MLM. Retail stores, shopping malls, catalogs, and most forms of advertising will soon be rendered obsolete by network marketing. At least, that's what you'll hear most MLM companies say.

Actually, fewer than 1 percent of all retail sales are made through MLM—and much of this consists of purchases by hopeful new distributors who are actually paying the price of admission to a business they will soon abandon. MLM is not replacing existing forms of marketing (though it's success can be enhanced by targeting social media marketing). In fact, it does not really compete with other marketing approaches at all. Rather, MLM represents a new investment proposition couched in the language of marketing. Its real products are distributorships. People are buying products to secure positions on the downline and the passive income that promises. The possibility is also floated that you may become rich—if not from your own efforts, then from the efforts of some unknown persons who might join your downline. So while MLM is not replacing traditional sales by any stretch, it does have a small footprint.

Promise 4: A Zen Lifestyle

MLM promises to be a new way of life that offers not only income, but happiness and fulfillment. It provides a way to attain all the good things that the world has to offer. Joining a company is not just a moneymaking venture, but a genuinely spiritual experience. It's like becoming part of a family. MLM is a positive, supportive new business that affirms the human spirit and personal freedom.

The most prominent motivational theme at MLM recruitment meetings is material success, followed by personal fulfillment with being your own "boss." Fortune 100 companies might blush at the excess of promises of wealth and luxury put forth by MLM solicitors because these appeals are often in conflict with people's true desire for meaningful and fulfilling work in which they have special talent or interest. However, more and more, MLM companies are packaging those promises together—that you can replace your day job by way of hustle and that you can find fulfillment in firing your boss. These ideas aren't mutually exclusive, and many companies are banking on it. By providing downline support, team building, and rewards (in addition to a paycheck), many companies try to make good on those dual promises. However, keep in mind that spiritual concepts like "prosperity consciousness" and "creative visualization" to promote MLM enrollment, the use of words like "communion" to describe a sales organization, and claims that MLM fulfills spiritual doctrines are very deceptive. When a product is wrapped in the flag or in religion, buyer beware! The "community" and "family" offered by MLM organizations to new recruits is based entirely upon their purchases. If the purchases and enrollment decline, so does the family.

Promise 5: The Perfect Job

Success in MLM will be easy, some promise, because your friends and relatives are natural prospects for sales. Those who love and support you will become your lifetime customers.

But the commercialization of family and friendship advocated in MLM marketing programs is a highly suspect and potentially destructive element for the individuals involved. Friends and family do not always appreciate being approached to buy products, especially if it happens more than once. It's one thing to buy Girl Scout cookies from your grandchild; it's another thing to buy a diet program from your sister-in-law. You may want to look elsewhere for customers and not mix business with family.

Promise 6: It's the Ultimate Side Hustle

You can do MLM in your spare time. As a business, it offers the greatest possible flexibility and personal freedom. A few hours a week can earn a significant passive income—which may eventually make any other work unnecessary.

But for most people, making money in MLM requires a serious time commitment, as well as considerable skill and persistence. Beyond the work and talent that's needed, the business model inherently infringes on areas of life that are not affected by most occupations. In MLM, everyone is a prospect. Every waking moment is a potential for marketing. There are no off-limit places, people, or times for selling. Consequently, there is no free space or free time once a person really buys into an MLM system. While claiming to offer independence, the system comes to dominate people's entire life and requires diligent adherence to the program.

Observers of the MLM phenomenon have noted the degree to which it seems to be fear-driven. Solicitations often include dire predictions about the impending collapse of other forms of distribution and the lack of opportunity in other occupations. Jobs outside MLM are demeaned for not offering unlimited income potential. In contrast to the disintegration or insensitivity of corporate America, MLM is presented as the last best hope for the American economy. Know that your goal is finding a truly passive income stream.

Promise 7: Freedom

Lastly, promise number seven: MLM is the best option for owning your own business and attaining real economic independence.

But does MLM constitute true self-employment? There's a strong argument that owning an MLM distributorship is an illusion. Many MLM companies forbid distributors to carry other companies' products. Most MLM contracts make termination of the distributorship easy and immediate for the company. Even short of termination, downlines can be taken away arbitrarily. Participation requires rigid adherence to a duplication model, not independence and individuality. It's possible to see MLM distributors not as entrepreneurs, but as joiners in a complex organization over which they have little control.

TOP TIPS FOR MLM SUCCESS

By Devlin Smith, *Entrepreneur* contributor

You probably have an image firmly planted in your mind of what network marketing (also known as direct sales or multilevel marketing) is all about—housewives buying and selling Tupperware while gossiping and eating finger sandwiches, or a high-pressure salesperson trying to convince you how easily you can become a millionaire if only you and your friends and their friends and so on would buy and sell vitamins with them.

Both of these images couldn't be further from the reality of network marketing. It's neither a hobby nor a get-rich scheme but an opportunity for you to earn money running your own part- or full-time business.

But what does it take to succeed in this industry? Vincent J. Kellsey, founder/CEO of Quantum Success Group, an organization that provides a variety of resources to women and men in the direct-selling industry, offers these seven tips for making it:

1. Choose Wisely

There are six key elements you should be looking for [when selecting an opportunity]. Number one: stability. How old is the company? Number two is excellent products or services that consumers will use and need more of.

Number three is the pay plan—how even and fair and generous overall is the distribution? This is really crucial, as the pay plan represents exactly how you'll get paid—or not get paid. There are really only two questions to ask: How many pennies out of each sales dollar get paid back to the distributors each month, and

TOP TIPS FOR MLM SUCCESS, CONTINUED

how fair is the distribution of these pennies between the old members and the new members?

Number four is the integrity of the company and the management. As much as possible, [investigate] the experience of the CEO, [their] experience in the network marketing industry, and their background. [Have] they been successful in other companies in the industry? Do they have a good reputation?

Number five is momentum and timing. Look at where the company's at, what's going on with the company, and if it's growing.

Number six is support, training, and business systems. You may have a great company with excellent management, products that make a difference, a pay plan that's uniquely fair and very generous, and momentum and stability, but if you don't have a system in place that works, all that [doesn't matter]. Most companies will have a transferable training system that they use, and that's where mentorship comes in.

2. Practice What They Preach

To succeed, you need to be willing to listen and learn from mentors. The way this industry is structured, it's in the best interests of the MLM veterans in your company to help you succeed, so they're willing to teach you the system. Whatever [your mentor] did to become successful, it's very duplicatable, but you have to be willing to listen and be taught and follow those systems.

3. Mind Your Upline

It can be called various things, but the general term is the "upline," meaning the people above you. How supportive are they? Do they call you? Do they help you put a plan in place? Are they

TOP TIPS FOR MLM SUCCESS, CONTINUED

as committed to your success as they are to their own? You should be able to relate to [the people in your upline] and be able to call them at any time to say "I need some help." How much support there is from the people above you in the company is very important.

4. Take the Lead with Your Downline

There's a term in the network marketing industry called "orphans"— when somebody is brought in, then the person who brought them in is just so busy bringing in other people that they don't spend the time to teach and train [the new person]. You should be prepared to spend at least 30 days helping a new person come into the industry—training them, supporting them, and holding their hand until they feel confident to be able to go off on their own. You really need to ask yourself if you are willing to do that. Are you able to do that? This is really about long-term relationship building. It's not about just bringing people into the business and just moving forward. It's about working with these people and helping them to develop relationships.

5. Get Online

People are using the internet (and social media in particular) as their main marketing tool. You can set up your site with autoresponders so when you capture leads, the autoresponder can follow up with that person. One of the greatest keys to success in this industry is follow-up. Many people will have someone call them who's interested, or they'll call the person and say they're interested, but then they don't follow up. Automation on the internet and social media has allowed a much more consistent method of following up. The only drawback with the internet is people who use it to

TOP TIPS FOR MLM SUCCESS, CONTINUED

spam. If there was one thing I could say [not to do] when using the internet as a marketing tool, it's spamming because that can give a very bad reputation not only to you, but also to the company you're working with.

6. Take Care of Business

This is a business, and just like if you were running a franchise or a storefront, you should have an accountant. You have all the same write-offs tax-wise that you have with running a business, so it's very important to [do your research] prior to getting involved, before you start making money from it. How is that going to affect you tax-wise? What are your write-offs? It's important to set up a [support] team around you. I'd suggest seeking out lawyers who deal in network marketing, so they're very versed in all the laws and how that affects [your business.]. There are also accountants who specialize in dealing with homebased businesses specifically in the direct selling industry.

7. Don't Quit Your Day Job . . . Yet

Never leave your full-time position unless you're absolutely certain that the income that's coming in with this company is going to be there. [Be sure that] you've been with the company [for a while] and that you know it's a stable company, and the income that you're earning is equal to or greater than the income you're earning from your job before quitting.

PARTING THOUGHTS

With all those promises and all those refutations in mind, let's conclude this chapter with three specific pieces of advice for getting involved with multilevel marketing. Remember, there are indeed people who have gained excellent passive income through network marketing. In addition, there are people who have become fabulously wealthy. You might be one of them. You might also be someone who can play tennis like Roger Federer or sing like Pavarotti. Or you might not be. Either way, please keep the following advice in mind.

First, avoid any compensation plan that includes commissions for recruiting more distributors. This is a red flag that could indicate an illegal pyramid. The company's emphasis should be on the income you can gain from selling the product, not the number of new people you can bring in. Be cautious of plans that claim you will make money through continued growth of your downline—that is, the number of distributors you recruit.

Second, beware of companies that ask new distributors to purchase expensive products and marketing materials. If the company claims to sell miracle products or promises enormous earnings, ask the promoter to substantiate those claims. Don't pay or sign any contracts in an "opportunity meeting" or any other pressure-filled situation. Insist on taking your time to think about your decision. Talk it over with a family member, friend, accountant, or lawyer.

Third and most important, do your homework! Check with your state's attorney general about any plan you're considering, especially when the claims about the product or your potential earnings seem too good to be true. Remember that no matter how good a product and how solid a multilevel marketing plan may be, you'll need to invest sweat equity as well as dollars for your investment to pay off. The fact is, it may indeed pay off, and it may pay off handsomely. But be aware that multilevel marketing is a high-risk means of building passive income.

This has been a largely cautionary chapter about a genuinely controversial channel for passive income. That's not to say that passive income success isn't achievable in MLM. It most certainly can be—but only if you've done your due diligence first and feel that the risk is truly worth the reward. In the next chapter, we'll look at the possibilities presented by licensing and franchising. These, too, have sometimes brought controversy— but they've also brought significant income to many people. As with MLM, you will need to decide for yourself.

OPENING DOORS WITH FRANCHISING

arlier, you read about creating passive income through the licensing of intellectual property, especially in the form of online content. In this chapter, you'll look at a special category of licensing called franchising. Chances are you have some knowledge of franchising already—but if you don't, you've missed one of the major transformations in the U.S. economy over the last 50 years. The history of McDonald's, for example, has become more than just a story—it's a full-fledged legend. How in the 1950s, Ray Kroc, a milkshake machine salesman, traveled to Riverside, California, to learn why a certain restaurant was selling so many milkshakes. What he found was a drive-in hamburger stand owned by the McDonald brothers. The brothers had perfected an assembly-line method of serving hamburgers that gave Kroc an idea—an idea, it turned out, that would have a huge effect on the American way of life. Kroc made a deal with the McDonald brothers that allowed him to open independently owned versions of the restaurant in other parts of the country. Plain and simple, it was a franchising deal—and the rest, as they say, is history.

Although the real history of McDonald's is a bit more complicated than the legend, the importance of franchising is certainly correct. Ray Kroc went on to become one of the wealthiest people in America, and the concept of franchising became one of the foundations of American business. That story has been told many times, and it's almost always told from Ray Kroc's point of view—that is, from the viewpoint of the franchisee. But what about the McDonald brothers? They were franchisors. For purposes of passive income, *their* role is the one we really need to look at.

What happened to the McDonald brothers can be described very simply. For a while, they received payments for the use of the McDonalds' name and the McDonalds' methods in drive-ins across the country. Ultimately, they were bought out by the company that Ray Kroc founded. Needless to say, they did very well in this transaction. They might have done vastly better if they had not been bought out, but that's a separate discussion. The point is, this was a successful example of franchising all around, and one that people have tried to duplicate ever since. Sometimes it's worked, and sometimes it hasn't. By the end of this chapter, you will have a good idea of what franchising is and how it can be used to generate passive income.

FRANCHISING 101

First, a definition: a franchise is a contract in which a franchisor licenses a name, a trademark, or a way of doing business to a franchisee. In exchange, the franchisor collects recurring payments— that is, passive income. The payments can be in the form of a flat annual fee, or a percentage of profits, or both. Sometimes, especially in large franchising operations, the franchisor provides advertising, training, and other support services. In turn, the franchisee must provide accurate financial records and must maintain certain standards of doing business.

Franchising has existed in America for more than a hundred years. Singer sewing machines, Coca-Cola distributorships, and Western Union telegraph offices were early examples of franchise businesses. Automobile dealerships were also franchise agreements between the manufacturers and local salespeople. But the food service industry is where franchising has really made its reputation. One of the first examples was Howard Johnson's, which began as a walk-up ice cream stand, and then later grew into a vast franchise of restaurants and hotels. In 1935, Howard Deering Johnson and Reginald Sprague established Howard Johnson's as the first full-service restaurant franchise. Independent operators used the Howard Johnson name, food, supplies, logo, and even building design—all in exchange for a fee.

The growth of franchises in the United States has not occurred without problems. As in multilevel marketing, some franchisors have focused more on the sale of franchises than on selling goods and services to the public. In some cases, franchisors made misrepresentations to franchisees, or failed to provide important information, or did not follow up with training and innovations. Because of this, and because of the large number of franchisee business failures that were taking place, legal remedies were put in place. Today, franchisors are required to furnish presale information to prospective buyers. At present, the problems once associated with franchising are definitely less prevalent, and franchising is recognized as an extremely powerful business model, both in America and around the world. For more information on the current rules governing franchises, check out the FTC's Franchise Rule site at www.ftc.gov/enforcement/rules/rulemaking-regulatory-reform-proceedings/franchise-rule.

But before we go any further, one basic point needs to be made. If you sell a license or franchise your business, the arrangement that results will not necessarily involve passive income. If, for example, you license computer software with the obligation to provide regular upgrades, you will have to keep working—unlike a stock market investment, in which all you have to do is track the ups and downs of your stocks. In this sense, franchising is more like real estate. You probably will not be able to completely disengage from the day-to-day operations of your franchisees. But to the extent that you are able to do that, franchising your business will come under the definition of creating passive income.

SHOULD YOU FRANCHISE?

Having said this, there is no doubt that franchising your business can have tremendous advantages. But before you begin the process of franchising, you must first determine if your concept and operating system are franchisable. Specifically, your business should meet the following criteria.

Credibility

First, your business should have credibility. You must be seen as both responsible and successful by prospective franchisees. They will have to earn enough profit after paying fees and royalties to gain an adequate return on investment—and if there isn't evidence that they can do that, they're not going to buy into your franchise.

Have a USP

Second, your business needs to be unique in some attractive way; it should have a unique selling proposition (USP). It must have sufficient differentiation from other franchises either in terms of products and services, marketing, lower investment cost, or target market. But this doesn't mean your business has to be unique in every way—because Pepsi is not totally different from Coke, nor is Burger King completely different from McDonald's. There's just enough difference so that customers are in a position to make a choice, and for the franchisee to influence them to make the right one.

Low Barriers to Entry

Third, your system and your business model should be relatively easy for a new franchisee to learn in a short time frame. Some businesses have been passed from parents to their children over many generations. They have an almost organic quality about them that is difficult to transfer to an outsider. This is not the kind of business that lends itself to franchising. If you are the founder of a business that has existed for only a few years, don't even think about franchising if you think of the company as "your baby." Because nobody else will feed and bathe your baby just the way you do—and that can only lead to trouble. In short, the basics of your business need to be transferable, and you have to be ready, willing, and able to pass them along.

Adaptability

Just as the structure of your business must be transferable, the physical realities of it should also not depend on a specific setting. Your concept should adapt well to many locations, and there should be widespread demand for your products or services. No aspect of lobster fishing is suited for franchising, because there just aren't that many places that have lobsters. Conversely, some of the best-known franchises have been successful precisely because their environment is transferable.

This was one of the truly inspired elements in McDonalds' success. During the late 1950s, air travel and the interstate highway system were just becoming staples of American life. People were traveling more than ever before, often with their families. When they were on the road and needed something to eat, it was reassuring to find a restaurant that was exactly like the one back home, down to the smallest detail. More recently, Starbucks has created a variation on the same theme. A customer who orders a drink with an elaborate Italian name at the Starbucks on the corner can get the exact same drink across the country. In this sense, both Starbucks and McDonald's are perfectly suited for franchising. Their sameness and uniformity may be the butt of jokes, but it's also made them a huge amount of money.

Without a doubt, the idea of franchising your business can be very exciting. Franchising multiplies and maximizes the profit-making potential of a proven business. If done effectively, it can provide a passive income stream that far surpasses the returns from a single-location enterprise. If all goes well, you will create a network of allied but semi-independent businesses—and they'll be bringing you passive income with every sale they make. Unlike multilevel marketing, this network will not depend on the downline recruiting of more and more distributors. Instead, the business model will be simple and traditional. When products or services are sold to the customers, everybody makes money—including you.

ENTREPRENEUR'S TEN QUESTIONS TO ASK WHEN FRANCHISING YOUR BUSINESS

Here are ten essential questions to ask when franchising your business:

1. *What are some resources I can look to as I start out?* Joel Libava, a professional franchise advisor in Cleveland and author of *Become a Franchise Owner!* (Wiley, 2011), suggests that you reach out to a franchise development company or a consultant who specializes in helping people franchise their businesses. They can boil the basics down for you fast, and some can also pair you with potential franchisees when you're ready. Bear in mind, however, that these are fee-based options that could cost you upwards of $50,000 to $100,000 each.

   The International Franchise Association (IFA) is another smart first stop for getting up to speed on franchising. The organization provides a wealth of helpful free and fee-based online educational resources.

2. *What are the ballpark startup costs involved?* Initial costs can range between $100,000 to $150,00 and often higher "to

TEN QUESTIONS, CONTINUED

really do it right, mainly in marketing, legal, and operations fees," says Libava. "Know from the outset that it's not cheap to turn your great business into a great franchise. This is no time to cut financial corners if you want to succeed."

Expect to fork over beaucoup bucks up front for everything from professional consultation fees, franchise location design, construction, and equipment. Then heap onto that paying for initial inventory and insurance. The list of expenses trails on.

3. *How much of a franchise royalty percentage should I collect?* Charging your franchisee a perpetual royalty percentage is generally how you'll make money from franchising. This is a pre-agreed upon cut of their gross sales—typically between 4 percent and 6 percent, though some franchise royalty fees climb as high as 25 percent. Libava says 5 percent is a "pretty normal royalty to charge for the privilege of using your brand and everything that entails."

Franchise royalty payments are typically collected on a monthly basis. You will also charge franchisees a one-time franchise fee, typically ranging between $30,000 to $35,000. The fee covers the cost of entry and purchasing a license to operate the business. Franchise fees can exceed $100,000 for advanced development deals and master franchises.

4. *How much do I stand to make?* There's no one-size-fits-all number. Profit margins will vary depending on how successful your franchise business becomes. However, to whet your appetite, Libava offers this scenario, which he says is fairly typical at the top of the franchising food chain: "If I'm a franchisor with 500 franchisees who each own one store, and

TEN QUESTIONS, CONTINUED

if every store does $500,000 a year in gross sales, and I'm getting 5 percent of that from each franchisee every year, I'd get $25,000 a year times 500. And, boom, that's $12.5 million in all, not a bad payday."

5. *What basic legal considerations do I need to be aware of?* Franchising is littered with complicated legal issues. It is best to consult with an experienced attorney whose area of expertise is franchise law. It's also important to note that certain states have registration requirements that you must comply with to legally franchise your business.

6. *What is a Franchise Disclosure Document, and why must I have one?* The FTC mandates that all franchisors provide prospective franchisees with a Franchise Disclosure Document (FDD) at least 14 days before partnering. It's a complex 23-section legal document, sometimes topping hundreds of pages and best completed by an attorney.

   The document informs franchisees of your company history and financials, about the various ins and outs of your franchise system (trademarks, patents, copyrights, etc.), and about the specific agreements and contracts franchisees are required to sign to buy in. FDDs—which typically cost between $10,000 and $35,000 to have drawn up—are designed to help franchisees make the most informed decision possible when considering investing in your franchise.

7. *How can I attract potential franchisees?* One of the best ways is to clearly explain within your company's various marketing materials and on your website what they stand to gain by investing in your brand. To further get the word out about

TEN QUESTIONS, CONTINUED

your franchising opportunity, you'll also want to set up booths at, and perhaps be present at, franchise industry trade shows like the International Franchise Expo.

You might also consider contracting with a franchise broker to generate franchisee leads for you. If they make a match that results in a sale, Mark Siebert, founder and CEO of iFranchise Group, a Homewood, Illinois-based franchising consultancy, says you can expect to pay them a fee between $10,000 and $15,000.

8. *How should I screen prospective franchisees?* "It's really hard as a new franchisor to turn down a $30,000 check from someone who has the money," Libava says, "but you have to be really careful. You have to interview them in person, get to know them, and make sure that they have the right look in their eyes."

To further establish trust—and to weed out bad apples ahead of time—Libava also recommends that you run background and credit checks on all potential franchisees. Be on the lookout for red flags like past lawsuits, fraud charges or convictions and bankruptcies.

9. *How many franchise locations should I open at first?* You have two choices here:

- You can opt for a single-unit (direct-unit) franchise, which is when you allow franchisees to operate one franchise location.

- You can offer franchisees multiunit arrangements, enabling them to run multiple franchise locations.

Both Libava and Siebert suggest that first-time franchisors bite off only one single-unit franchise operation. If your

TEN QUESTIONS, CONTINUED

inaugural franchise effort earns enough profit to make the venture worthwhile, and you're comfortable with the amount hard work involved, only then should you consider adding additional units.

10. *What are some common rookie mistakes to avoid?* Libava says the worst mistake he's seen is consulting with a franchise attorney only, without seeking the additional advice of a franchise development firm or consultant. "It's called being cheap and it can really cost you in the long run, sometimes your entire operation."

Another common blunder is turning your business into a franchise without opening a second guinea pig location first, he says. "That's your prototype location, how you see if franchising is even doable for you in the first place."

GET YOUR DUCKS IN A ROW

Certain things need to be in place before you can even begin to think about franchising. First and foremost, your own business has to be well-established and successful. The bottom line has to be very solid, not just this year but over the course of a substantial history. Also, for franchising to be worthwhile, expanding your business should be inherently exciting to you. It should not be just about more money or increased profitability. If that's all you're interested in, you can probably become more profitable by laying off employees than by taking on new partners.

Think hard about these issues, and see what other issues come up in your mind. It may be that your business is a good candidate for franchising right now. But even if your business is not quite ready to take the leap into franchising right now, there are things you can do now to prepare for franchising down the road.

Check Your ROI

For example, we've already mentioned the need to demonstrate consistent returns on investment (ROI). Profitability is always a determining factor in the success or failure of franchising. Franchise investors want to put their money in a venture that offers a guaranteed return—or as close to a guarantee as possible. That's why they are willing to pay franchise fees of $100,000 or more. In exchange, it is not unusual for franchise investors to expect a 20 percent annual return. And they expect to see solid reasons to support that expectation.

Secure Your Systems

You also need to have proven and well-documented operating systems in place. Efficiency is the key to running an effective franchise. Successfully franchised businesses have fine-tuned their operational procedures, which are supported by practical and comprehensive operations manuals. Franchise investors don't want to reinvent the wheel to find out what works.

Test Multiple Locations

Also, before you decide to venture into the world of franchising, you should probably have opened more than one location for your business already. The lessons you learn are a preview of what you'll encounter in full-scale franchising. You'll also begin to understand which geographic locations hold the best potential for future franchises. More important, multiple locations will demonstrate to potential investors that your business concept is transportable and capable of prospering in more than one market.

Build Your Team

Grooming key employees is another basic need. Long before you make the decision to franchise your business, you should have a team of people in place who can make it all work. These employees should have a deep understanding of your business's operating systems as well as the ability to communicate their knowledge to others. You might want to identify a few outstanding employees and involve them in preparing an operations manual for future franchisees. This can be an extremely useful and informative project, even if you don't actually get into franchising until far in the future.

With all this in mind, let's meet three business owners who are considering franchising. As you read their stories, ask yourself whether or not their companies seem like good franchise prospects. More specifically, ask whether you yourself would like to own one of the franchises. And if the answer is no, what would have to change in order for your no to become a yes?

LENA'S STORY

Since I was a teenager, I've always worked in restaurants. First I was a waitress, and then I started spending more time in the kitchen. Eventually I became a chef and had jobs in a few very high-end establishments. But I was always fascinated by food preparation at all different levels. Once I even thought of opening a place that served nothing but variations on peanut butter sandwiches, which I still think is a good idea. If you disagree, try researching the amount of peanut butter Americans eat every year. You may want to steal my idea.

But instead of peanut butter sandwiches, I wound up with a concept that may seem even more mundane. One day at home, just for fun, I started experimenting with ways of making prepackaged toasted sandwiches in a regular toaster. In other words, if you want to make a grilled cheese and tomato sandwich, you can just put the packet into the toaster and heat it up. You don't have to actually put the sandwich together every time you want to eat one. This can save a lot of time, because you can't really make a grilled cheese sandwich or a tuna melt or a BLT in a microwave. Anyway, this was something I learned how to do, and then I decided to test it. I set up a booth at a big art fair near my house, and in one day I sold more than a hundred packets. I knew my instinct had been right.

Based on my experience, I knew how to talk to owners of small shops and restaurants—and I knew which ones could move this product. So I started selling into a number of places in my home town, especially places that did a big lunch business for people in a hurry. I also knew the importance of displaying the items well, so I provided the shops with ways of displaying the product attractively. Finally—and again because of my background in restaurants—I knew that some of the smaller places would be slow to pay. So, I targeted the ones that I knew would pay on time, which was crucial to survival in the early days.

After a year, I had more than 100 accounts for my packaged meals. But the ones that did best weren't actually full-fledged restaurants. They were stalls or pushcarts in malls and other public spaces. In fact, some of these accounts wanted to go over to selling nothing but my products. At lunchtime, there would be lines of people, and the toasted sandwiches were all they wanted to buy.

That's when the possibility of franchising first came into my mind— and I thought more seriously about it when I had my second baby. My products had been selling for about two years, and the demand was still strong. In fact, my biggest priority became coming up with a broader range of products. But I also want to spend more time with my family, so franchising is starting to look like a really solid possibility.

Lena's business would seem to be an ideal candidate for franchising. The concept has already proved itself over a substantial period of time and in multiple locations. The costs involved are relatively small, so if a particular location doesn't work out, her exit strategy will be simple. One problem might be gaining proprietary rights to the process of creating the packaged meals. If the business is as successful as it has been so far, it won't be long before competitors start appearing— especially since, once it's understood, the process seems to be quite simple. This question is one the business owner should take up with an attorney, because it's a question potential partners are sure to ask.

ANNA'S STORY

When I was a growing up, I always loved horses. I was never able to have my own horse, but my parents enrolled me in a riding academy, and I spent a lot of time there. I got to know the horses so well that it was almost as if they belonged to me. I also loved to draw horses, or read about them, or watch movies about them. And I made friends with a lot of other kids who felt the same way.

After college I became a teacher in a middle school, and I noticed that there were a certain number of girls who were just the way I had been. I'd be talking to the class, and they'd be sitting there drawing horses. The surprising thing was, these girls were always very good students, just as I had been. It was really a very distinct personality type.

Meanwhile, my own interest in horses had by no means gone away. I got a weekend job with a top trainer who owned a riding academy like the one I had attended as a girl. From her I learned all aspects of running a really outstanding yard.

After working with this trainer for several years, I decided to set up my own business. I would specialize in training preteens and teenagers to ride horses up to competition standard. This involved a big financial investment. Training horses and training kids to ride them isn't something you can do in your backyard unless you've got a very big backyard. To help get a grip on this, I enrolled in business school part time. My instructor in a business startup course helped me draw up an initial business plan. Based on the plan and my solid background, I was able to purchase an existing facility. It needed an upgrade, but it also had a lot of potential.

Very quickly this business literally took over my life. I had no problem at all building up a clientele, but there were times when I felt over-whelmed. I had to deal with administration, finance, and marketing as well as the core business. I wasn't prepared for the amount of paperwork involved, particularly in relation to employees. Still, the one thing I never had to worry about was getting customers. There's a lot of interest in this on the part of many kids, and there are very few outlets for that interest.

Recently I had the idea of trying to brand or franchise my riding academy in the way that others have done with health clubs and fitness centers. Obviously in a given city there are only so many riding academies you can have. But I think you could have a number of them across the country, and this would become the place to go for kids who are interested in horses. I haven't looked into it in any detail, but the concept of expanding in that way definitely seems interesting.

Unfortunately, this business seems to be the mirror image of the prepackaged meals we discussed a moment ago. It's hard to think of a more labor-intensive, high-investment, high-maintenance enterprise than a riding academy. As the owner says, there is a large customer base waiting to be served—but the expenses of serving it are huge. There are also other issues to consider here that don't exist in the average retail business. Insurance will be a significant cost for franchisees—and in light of this, it will be important to find highly trained and competent employees. That might not be easy, and it might not be cheap. All in all, this business sounds like a labor of love for the owner, and labors of love are not easily transferable to multiple locations. Neither are horses, for that matter.

WILL'S STORY

Most people who start their own businesses are creative individuals and they have a fairly high tolerance for risk. They're not exactly dreamers, but they do have imagination. They're not comfortable with the idea of just doing one thing for the rest of their lives, even though that one thing might bring them financial security. They're more interested in freedom than security.

For those kinds of people, accounting is not exactly a turn-on. They know that a new business needs to affiliate with an accountant, but that's about all they know. It's not really something they want to think about. They like to focus on marketing or developing their product, and they just want somebody else to look after the numbers.

As a CPA with my own small firm, I did some research and saw that most accountants offer the same basic package, such as tax planning and payroll services. Although I was confident that our services were some of the best around, I wanted to get a competitive edge in an increasingly tough market. So, two years ago I launched a specialist small-business development service aimed at entrepreneurs. This new service has really increased our profitability per customer and boosted our business volumes.

From talking to prospective clients, I realized that many new business owners need specialized help, but they don't know who to go to and who to trust. They tend to be wary of anyone who describes himself or herself as a general business consultant. They think that they'll get lost among the accountant's larger clients and not get any personalized attention. By listening to feedback, we identified a market for a trusted business-development service. We also researched our competitors and found that there were no other practices in our area offering a similar service.

In launching our business-development branch, the fact that we already had five offices was an advantage. We were big enough to be credible, but not too big. It's true that all diversification strategies carry some risk, but we wanted to minimize that risk by limiting the resources we committed to the project. We got the job done, it's been successful, and we also learned a lot. If I did it again, I'd take a bolder approach. For example, a launch event of some kind would have been a good start to an initial marketing push.

Fortunately, or unfortunately, I don't have to do it over again. But we have been thinking of creating a franchise for accounting services along the lines of H&R Block tax preparation. The target audience would be freelancers, startups, and small business owners. I think this is an idea that has a lot of potential.

This seems like an excellent possibility for franchising. The target clientele has been identified, and the owner has a clear understanding of exactly what customers are going to want. Moreover, the business has already proved itself in multiple locations. Startup costs can be very low, depending on the location of the offices, and the H&R Block comparison is an excellent one. In fact, the possibility of a buyout by a major corporation could be a huge upside. H&R Block was long ago bought by Sears, and that fact could create an exciting scenario for possible franchisees.

THE NINE ADVANTAGES OF FRANCHISING

By Mark Siebert, author of *Franchise Your Business* and *The Franchisee Handbook*

The primary advantages for most companies entering the realm of franchising are capital, speed of growth, motivated management, and risk reduction—but there are many others as well.

1. Capital

The most common barrier to expansion faced by today's small businesses is lack of access to capital. Even before the credit-tightening of 2008-2009 and the new normal that ensued, entrepreneurs often found that their growth goals outstripped their ability to fund them.

Franchising, as an alternative form of capital acquisition, offers some advantages. The primary reason most entrepreneurs turn to franchising is that it allows them to expand without the risk of debt or the cost of equity. First, since the franchisee provides all the capital required to open and operate a unit, it allows companies

NINE ADVANTAGES, CONTINUED

to grow using the resources of others. By using other people's money, the franchisor can grow largely unfettered by debt.

Moreover, since the franchisee—not the franchisor—signs the lease and commits to various contracts, franchising allows for expansion with virtually no contingent liability, thus greatly reducing the risk to the franchisor. This means that as a franchisor, not only do you need far less capital with which to expand, but your risk is largely limited to the capital you invest in developing your franchise company—an amount that is often less than the cost of opening one additional company-owned location.

2. Motivated Management

Another stumbling block facing many entrepreneurs wanting to expand is finding and retaining good unit managers. All too often, a business owner spends months looking for and training a new manager, only to see them leave or, worse yet, get hired away by a competitor. And hired managers are only employees who may or may not have a genuine commitment to their jobs, which makes supervising their work from a distance a challenge.

But franchising allows the business owner to overcome these problems by substituting an owner for the manager. No one is more motivated than someone who is materially invested in the success of the operation. Your franchisee will be an owner—often with their life's savings invested in the business. And their compensation will come largely in the form of profits.

The combination of these factors will have several positive effects on unit level performance.

&— *Long-term commitment.* Since the franchisee is invested, they will find it difficult to walk away from their business.

NINE ADVANTAGES, CONTINUED

☙ *Better-quality management.* As a long-term "manager," your franchisee will continue to learn about the business and is more likely to gain institutional knowledge of your business that will make them a better operator as they spend years, maybe decades, of their life in the business.

☙ *Improved operational quality.* While there are no specific studies that measure this variable, franchise operators typically take the pride of ownership very seriously. They will keep their locations cleaner and train their employees better because they own, not just manage, the business.

☙ *Innovation.* Because they have a stake in the success of their business, franchisees are always looking for opportunities to improve their business—a trait most managers don't share.

☙ *Franchisees typically out-manage managers.* Franchisees will also keep a sharper eye on the expense side of the equation—on labor costs, theft (by both employees and customers), and any other line item expenses that can be reduced.

☙ *Franchisees typically outperform managers.* Over the years, both studies and anecdotal information have confirmed that franchisees will outperform managers when it comes to revenue generation. Based on our experience, this performance improvement can be significant—often in the range of 10 to 30 percent.

3. Speed of Growth

Every entrepreneur I've ever met who's developed something truly innovative has the same recurring nightmare: that someone else will beat them to the market with their own concept. And often these fears are based on reality.

NINE ADVANTAGES, CONTINUED

The problem is that opening a single unit takes time. For some entrepreneurs, franchising may be the only way to ensure that they capture a market leadership position before competitors encroach on their space, because the franchisee performs most of these tasks. Franchising not only allows the franchisor financial leverage, but also allows it to leverage human resources as well. Franchising allows companies to compete with much larger businesses so they can saturate markets before these companies can respond.

4. Staffing Leverage

Franchising allows franchisors to function effectively with a much leaner organization. Since franchisees will assume many of the responsibilities otherwise shouldered by the corporate home office, franchisors can leverage these efforts to reduce overall staffing.

5. Ease of Supervision

From a managerial point of view, franchising provides other advantages as well. For one, the franchisor is not responsible for the day-to-day management of the individual franchise units. At a micro level, this means that if a shift leader or crew member calls in sick in the middle of the night, they're calling your franchisee— not you—to let them know. And it's the franchisee's responsibility to find a replacement or cover their shift. And if they choose to pay salaries that aren't in line with the marketplace, employ their friends and relatives, or spend money on unnecessary or frivolous purchases, it won't impact you or your financial returns. By eliminating these responsibilities, franchising allows you to direct your efforts toward improving the big picture.

NINE ADVANTAGES, CONTINUED

6. Increased Profitability

The staffing leverage and ease of supervision mentioned above allows franchise organizations to run in a highly profitable manner. Since franchisors can depend on their franchisees to undertake site selection, lease negotiation, local marketing, hiring, training, accounting, payroll, and other human resources functions (just to name a few), the franchisor's organization is typically much leaner (and often leverages off the organization that's already in place to support company operations). So, the net result is that a franchise organization can be more profitable.

Unfortunately, it is difficult to quantify or prove this contention. This much we do know: Research done during the past 10 years shows top quartile franchisors put an average of 40 and 45.6 percent to the bottom line in 2001 and 2002, respectively. How many industries can you think of where net incomes in this range are even possible?

7. Improved Valuations

The combination of faster growth, increased profitability, and increased organizational leverage helps account for the fact that franchisors are often valued at a higher multiple than other businesses. So, when it comes time to sell your business, the fact that you're a successful franchisor that has established a scalable growth model could certainly be an advantage.

When the iFranchise Group compared the valuation of the S&P 500 vs. the franchisors tracked in Franchise Times magazine in 2012, the average price/earnings ratio of franchise companies was 26.5, while the average P/E ratio of the S&P 500 was 16.7.

NINE ADVANTAGES, CONTINUED

This represents a staggering 59 percent premium to the S&P. Moreover, more than two-thirds of the franchisors surveyed beat the S&P ratio.

8. Penetration of Secondary and Tertiary Markets

The ability of franchisees to improve unit-level financial performance has some weighty implications. A typical franchisee will not only be able to generate higher revenues than a manager in a similar location but will also keep a closer eye on expenses. Moreover, since the franchisee will likely have a different cost structure than you do as a franchisor (she may pay lower salaries, may not provide the same benefits packages, etc.), they can often operate a unit more profitably even after accounting for the royalties they must pay you.

As a franchisor, this can give you the flexibility to consider markets in which corporate returns might be marginal. Of course, you never want to consider a market you don't feel provides the franchisee with a strong likelihood of success. But if your strategy involves developing corporate units in addition to franchising, you'll likely find your limited capital development budget won't allow you to open as many locations as you'd like. Franchisees, on the other hand, could open and operate successfully in markets that are not high on your priority list for development.

9. Reduced Risk

By its very nature, franchising also reduces risk for the franchisor. Unless you choose to structure it differently (and few do), the franchisee has all the responsibility for the investment in the franchise operation, paying for any build-out, purchasing any

NINE ADVANTAGES, CONTINUED

inventory, hiring any employees, and taking responsibility for any working capital needed to establish the business.

The franchisee is also the one who executes leases for equipment, autos, and the physical location, and has the liability for what happens within the unit itself, so you're largely out from under any liability for employee litigation (e.g., sexual harassment, age discrimination, EEOC), consumer litigation (the hot coffee spilled in your customer's lap), or accidents that occur in your franchise (slip-and-fall, employer's comp, etc.).

Moreover, it's very likely that your attorney and other advisors will suggest you create a new legal entity to act as the franchisor. This will further limit your exposure. And since the cost of becoming a franchisor is often less than the cost of opening one more location (or entering one more market), your startup risk is greatly reduced.

The combination of these factors provides you with substantially reduced risk. Franchisors can grow to hundreds or even thousands of units with limited investment and without spending any of their own capital on unit expansion.

PARTING THOUGHTS

If you do get started in franchising, you'll quickly learn that you've entered a new enterprise—with all the possibilities and challenges that doing that includes. Regardless of the exact nature of your business, you'll have at least two roles: selling the franchises, then servicing the franchises. Of the two, ensuring the success of your franchisees is more important. So, make sure you're prepared for this. Be aware that franchise holders are much more like partners or shareholders than like employees.

chapter eleven ▪ opening doors with franchising

They can provide you with a great passive income stream, but it will never be completely passive on your end. As we've said, franchising is more like real estate investing than like putting your money in the stock market. It's also a bit like gardening. You'll want to grow your franchises the way other people grow roses. Once you're sure that your business is ready to franchise, the key to success is successful franchisees. Without them, no franchise system can last. With them, you might become the next McDonald's—or would you prefer a Burger King?

CHAPTER TWELVE

CREATING A PASSIVE INCOME LEGACY

Now, we're going to be looking at how you can create a legacy of passive income. What does legacy mean? Well, in this case, it's income that will persist far into the future. This is a path that extends beyond the edges of our map into the realm of the future. When you follow this path, the income contribution you're making now will go on—even after you're no longer contributing.

If this doesn't exactly sound like a barrel of laughs, please bear with us. The material we're going to cover in this chapter is extremely important. Most people who have achieved financial success devote serious attention to how that success can be perpetuated—and in this chapter we'll look at some of the best ways for bringing that about. It's interesting also that at least a few very successful investors have renounced the whole idea of leaving a legacy, or at least one that can be put in a bank account. For these individuals, the best gift to their heirs is the chance for them to start over all by themselves if not quite from scratch, then from pretty close to it.

The best-known proponent of this belief is Warren Buffett, the icon of stock market investing and one of the world's wealthiest people. Buffett has long been an advocate of low taxation, with one important exception. He would support an inheritance tax of 100 percent. That way, everyone starts life on a level playing field, no matter what the person's parents and grandparents might have done. In theory at least, this would ensure that everyone tries harder and the entire society benefits.

Actually, there have been varying reports of how far Warren Buffett wants to go with this. He may not advocate the complete elimination of inheritance, but he definitely wants to limit it. He has often said that wealthy parents should leave their children with enough money to have what they want, but not enough so they do nothing at all. He has pledged a $31 billion-legacy to the Bill and Melinda Gates Foundation—a tidy sum that will be going outside his family forever—as well as another $6 billion to other charitable foundations. As a result, Warren Buffett has opened a fundamental debate about the concept of financial legacy. Is it better to limit what you pass on and not spoil your heirs or to let them inherit the wealth and build on it?

THE GIFT OF A PLAN

While the majority of affluent Americans age 45 and older intend to leave an inheritance to their families, one in four has not yet made any plans to do so. Much has been written about the eventual transfer of $41 trillion in wealth from the baby boom generation. This transfer will definitely take place, but it may not go where the boomers intend. Instead, it may go to the IRS. This is what's going to happen unless more attention is given to planning alternatives. Ironically, 70 percent of individuals planning to leave a financial legacy cite the impact of estate taxes as their biggest concern.

Two-thirds of those who do not have any plan say "I intend to. I just haven't gotten around to it yet." The main reason given for not having a legacy plan—or even a will—is a very simple one: procrastination. Laziness might be another word. Or denial. Surprisingly, the number-two reason given for not having a plan is "my estate is too small"—even in a study in which the average net worth of subjects was almost $2 million.

Yet most people definitely need estate planning, especially if there's a desire to provide passive income. Typically, the older you get, the more assets you acquire, and the more complicated your affairs become. Without a legacy plan, your most personal decisions about where your assets go could be determined by others. Your heirs could also face legal obstacles and tax burdens derived from this confusion—not to mention some intense family strife.

THE ROLE OF CHARITABLE GIVING AND GIFT TAXES

Studies have also uncovered some surprising findings related to charitable giving. When asked if they would leave all or part of their estate to charities, universities, or nonprofit organizations, only 10 percent of affluent Americans over the age of 45 said that they are likely to do so. Of the 56 percent who are not at all likely to leave anything to charity, many say they don't trust that their money would be well spent. Others simply can't think of any organizations to which they want to leave money—and the vast majority intend to leave an estate to their children instead.

From the perspective of a legacy, it's important to look at charitable giving for several reasons. First, it can, of course, make a positive difference in the general quality of life—but giving to charity can also reduce the amount of estate tax that must be paid. The size of this tax will naturally affect the size of whatever else is in an estate. Yet estate taxes on a legacy are stated in almost three-quarters of people age 45 or older. In fact, 80 percent of affluent Americans in this age group believe that estate taxes should be eliminated completely.

Besides charitable giving, another underutilized element in legacy planning is the gift tax provision. While most people are vaguely aware that something of this nature exists, less than a third of them have actually taken advantage of it. Of those who either aren't aware or who haven't gifted yet, 59 percent say that they are likely to in the future. But that's what they say about all aspects of legacy planning. They intend to do it, but they just haven't gotten around to it—which may be another way of saying they intend to live forever.

WHAT DOES LEGACY LOOK LIKE?

Often, legacy issues can become vehicles for magical thinking among a substantial number of people. The focus is no longer just dollars and cents, but power, influence, and the continuation of life itself. As you read earlier in the book, the power of passive income is the ability to build a wealth of time and freedom, thanks to passive income that you don't have to actively trade your time for.

So, what do people think their heirs will do with the money? Most of those who expect to leave a legacy think it will be a cushion for their children's futures—something basically unnecessary but nice to have. In contrast, most of the potential recipients believe they could definitely use help with their day-to-day expenses, or help to fund their own eventual retirements.

Contrary to what many potential givers may suspect, receiving a legacy rarely leads to splurge behavior or laziness. Only 5 percent of those who anticipate receiving a legacy say they plan to make a once-in-a-lifetime splurge or work less. Of those who have already received money, the majority have not treated it frivolously. The most frequent uses of the legacy include paying for children's education, maintaining a lifestyle in the face of rising costs, or creating a new legacy that can be passed along in turn.

It's interesting that more than 50 percent of affluent Americans age 45 and older received a legacy themselves at some point in their lives.

About half who have lost one or both of their parents have received an inheritance from them. One in three has received an inheritance from relatives other than parents—and some are still waiting to do so. Of those with one or both parents still living, seven out of ten anticipate receiving a legacy. Legacy looks different for each generation, and the meaning shifts over time, as Jack shares below:

> *I joined the army when I was 16 years old. I said I was 17 and that's how I got in. It was the start of World War II, and they weren't asking too many questions. When the war ended, I found that the country had changed a great deal from when I was growing up in the Depression. And I must say, it was a lot better. Based on my service in the military, I was able to go to college for nothing. Later I was able to get a loan on my first house on very favorable terms. It's true that I didn't inherit anything from my parents at all, but I did get a different kind of inheritance from my Uncle Sam. I try to remember that when I start to think that everybody has it easier today. In a lot of ways, they do have it easier. They're not standing in lines to get a cup of soup like in the 1930s. But they're also not getting a free ride from the government about things like education for their kids.*

As Jack's story shows, times have changed and most of us facing retirement can no longer rely on government programs or built-in pension programs. More and more people are looking to family legacies to help ease the burden on their loved ones as they, too, age and face uncertain economic conditions. It can be a tricky topic, no matter what your legacy plans are. Subjects such as leaving and/or receiving a legacy can be emotional for family members—but most people do agree that it can be very beneficial. Research shows that almost everyone who has indeed talked with their parents about legacy plans feels it was a positive experience: All were happy to know their parents' intentions, even if they didn't agree with them. On the other hand, a high proportion of older people were uncomfortable with discussing this. Some of their reasons were: "I don't want anybody to count on the money" or "I want my heirs to be pleasantly surprised" or "I intend to talk about it when I'm older."

But reasons like this are just different versions of procrastination or denial. To move beyond this, let's look at some of the practical issues of creating a passive income legacy. It's a complex subject but a very important one—and, fortunately, there are also some surprisingly simple solutions.

BUILD YOUR PASSIVE INCOME LEGACY

Regardless of where you stand on this issue, there's a lot to consider. As your income grows, you should think seriously about how—or whether—you want to perpetuate it. One thing is certain: You need to have a plan for your money. Or rather, you need to have several plans covering the present, the near-term future, and the long-term future.

This may seem like a daunting task when you first start to think about it, but financial planning doesn't have to be difficult. It begins with four questions to ask yourself—and you should ask them not just once but at least twice a year because you may find that your answers change. The four questions are these:

1. Where do you want to be financially?
2. How much time do you have to get there?
3. Where are you now?
4. What vehicles give you a chance to get there on time?

Let's look at these one by one.

Where Do You Want to Be?

First, where do you want to be in financial terms? Setting a financial goal is no different than choosing a travel destination. You're trying to get somewhere with your money. You're trying to reach a certain goal—and knowing your goal means everything in money management. If you don't know where you want to be, you won't know how to get there. And you won't know how to avoid or minimize the risks along the way. You may not even recognize the risks at all.

Second, how much time do you have to get where you want to be? The time you have to reach your financial destination will determine the level of urgency you feel. Again, it's like planning a trip. Once you see how far you have to go, you may be comfortable with the time you have to get there—or you may need to give yourself more time—or you may need to adjust your goal to meet your deadline.

What Is Your Timeline?

Time is a huge factor in investing. The relationship between your time and your objective will always play a role in your planning. If you have five hours to travel 500 miles, you're going to think about planning your trip differently than if you have five hours to travel only a tenth of that distance. It's the same with money. You have to know how far you need to go and in what time frame. That's the only way to create an intelligent plan for getting there.

Where Are You Now?

Where are you now in your financial life? How much money can you put toward your goal at this moment? What's your starting point? The answer to this comes in two parts: your net worth, which is the total value of everything you own, minus the debts you have to repay, and your monthly cash flow, which shows your monthly income and spending patterns. It's a snapshot of how money flows into and out of your life. When this information is clear in your mind, you can start making informed decisions. If you want to create a passive income legacy of $200,000, for example, you'll be able to see how much money you can designate toward this goal right now. You might have $25,000 in a retirement plan and $15,000 in a savings account. You don't want to touch your retirement savings—but perhaps you can move some money from your savings into a vehicle that will benefit your heirs.

How Will You Get There?

What financial vehicles will let you meet your goals in the time available? When you plan a trip, you need to know how far you have to travel and how long you have to get there. Once you have that information, choosing the vehicle and the route should be obvious. Investment and estate planning decisions can be clear, too. You just have to know your legacy goals and be familiar with the vehicles that can get you there.

LIFE INSURANCE

One of the most important vehicles you have to help you achieve your long-term financial goals is life insurance. This may not sound very creative or exciting, but life insurance really is an extremely effective way to provide a legacy for your heirs. Since there are several different kinds of insurance and the benefits come in different forms, please listen carefully to what we're about to say. It can save you money and also increase the money that your heirs will eventually receive.

Life insurance provides funds for your family—or actually for anyone you designate—after you're gone. The person you designate is called the beneficiary. There are no restrictions on how the beneficiary can use the money—whether it's to pay debt, the cost of the funeral, estate taxes, college tuition, or any anticipated expense.

Basically, there are two categories of life insurance coverage. Individual coverage pertains to you alone and is bought by you either through a broker or directly from an insurance company. You may also be able to buy group coverage if it's offered by your employer or another organization. Generally, group coverage is cheaper because of the group rates.

Explore Your Policy Options

Within the two categories of group or individual coverage, there are also two basic kinds of policies: term insurance and permanent insurance. The first of these pays off if you die within a specific period of time—which is the term of the policy. Like auto and homeowner's insurance, term insurance covers you only during the time you're making payments. For this reason, it's less expensive than permanent life insurance. There are three different varieties of term insurance:

1. Convertible term insurance lets you convert the policy into a permanent one at any time. There's no medical exam, but premiums may go up as you age.

2. Level term insurance lets you pay the same premium every year for the length of the term. Your beneficiaries are entitled to the same payoff if you die at any time during the term. If you want to renew your policy at the end of the term, your premium may rise significantly because you'll be considerably older.

3. Last, decreasing term insurance pays a death benefit that gradually goes down in value over time. Premiums usually remain the same throughout the term.

Permanent insurance is generally more expensive than term. Unlike term insurance, the permanent variety continues in force until you die, as long as you make timely payments. It may also include a savings feature that builds up a cash reserve you can use while you're alive. In fact, if there's enough in the reserve, you can use the cash to pay the premiums. There are also three varieties of permanent insurance:

1. First, whole life lets you pay a fixed premium for a fixed death benefit. There is a cash savings feature that, over time, provides you with a cash reserve.

2. The second variety, universal life, is a little more flexible. You may be able to change the amount of insurance as your needs change. Some changes may require a medical exam.

3. Third, variable life invests some of your premiums in stocks, bonds, and money market funds. The upside is that your investments may perform well and provide a larger cash reserve. The downside is the risk that the investments will lose money. Sometimes a minimum cash value for the policy is guaranteed, but this is unusual. Most insurers guarantee a minimum death benefit, although it may not be what you had hoped to receive. Variable-universal life combines the premium and death benefit flexibility of universal life with the investment flexibility and risk of variable life insurance.

Choose Your Type

So what kind of insurance is best? Fortunately, for most people there's a very simple one-word answer to that question. Term is best. But before we explain why, it's important to look in a bit closer at the differences between term and whole life, which is the most popular kind of permanent insurance.

The basic difference is this: A term policy is life coverage only. On the death of the insured, it pays the face amount of the policy to the named beneficiary. You can buy term for periods of one year up to 30 years. Whole life insurance, on the other hand, combines a term policy with an investment component. The investment could be in bonds and money-market instruments or stocks. The policy builds cash value that you can borrow against.

Whole life insurance is expensive partly because you're also paying for the investment portion. That extra cost might almost be worth it if these policies were a good investment vehicle. But usually they aren't. Insurance agents like to call these policies retirement plans—but leaving aside the fact that there are many better ways to save for retirement, these policies come with high fees and commissions—and these costs are deducted from the annual return. On top of that, there are upfront commissions that are typically 100 percent of your first year's premium. Even worse, it's often impossible to tell what the return on the investment will be—or how much of what you pay in goes toward the insurance and how much toward the investment. Another problem with whole life that is only an expert can tell if a policy you own or are considering will ever become a decent investment. Whole life policies hardly ever yield a reasonable return unless held for 20 years or more. So if you buy one, be prepared to pay into it for the long haul.

Premiums for term insurance are downright cheap for people in good health up to about age 50. After that age, premiums start to get progressively more expensive. The same holds true for whole life policies, although people who need coverage in their 60s and beyond may have no alternative but to buy whole life. Most companies won't sell term policies to people over age 65.

This has been complex information, but it's also very valuable. If you're not sure you've understood it all, here's an easy way to get the gist of it. The secret is in the phrase "whole life." Never buy it in your whole life! That's really all you need to know.

CONSIDER A TRUST

Life insurance can definitely be a passive income resource, but who will benefit from that resource is not always clear. For example, if you are the insured and you are the owner of the policy, the proceeds of the policy will be subject to estate tax when you die. But if you transfer ownership to a life insurance trust, the proceeds will be completely free of estate tax.

The estate tax (sometimes referred to as the "death tax") varies based on the amount of the gift. As of this writing, the rate ranges from 18 percent for gifts under $10,000 up to 40 percent for gifts exceeding $1 million. So a life insurance trust can save hundreds of thousands of dollars for a substantial estate. However, there are several drawbacks to such an arrangement.

Inflexibility

For example, you can't change the beneficiary of the policy. In fact, the trust itself is legally the beneficiary. The trustee alone has that right, and you cannot serve as trustee of your own life insurance trust. Of course, you will designate the beneficiaries of the trust. But because this designation cannot be changed after the life insurance trust has been set up, you will lack the flexibility to deal with changed family circumstances with this particular policy.

Irrevocability

Second, the life insurance trust must be irrevocable. Once you have set up and funded the trust, you cannot get the policy back. If you become uninsurable owing to a health issue, you will be committed to this trust as your only life insurance.

Requires a Trustee

Third, you must find or hire a trustee. Again, you can't serve as trustee of your life insurance trust. That means that you will have to find or hire a third-party trustee—which is often the bank where the trust is located. Fortunately, many banks and trust companies offer reduced fees for life insurance trusts because they involve essentially no investing decisions.

Despite these drawbacks, many people find that the tax-saving potential of a life insurance trust is worth the extra effort. It allows you to remove from your estate a significant asset that you are unlikely to want access to during your life. And it ensures that the life insurance proceeds go 100 percent to your beneficiaries, not to the federal government. Consult a banker or an attorney for more information on legacy planning in general and insurance trusts in particular.

PARTING THOUGHTS

We've now seen some of the obstacles that people put on the path toward creating a legacy. Hopefully, we've also seen how important it is to get past those obstacles. The problems start when we bring psychological or emotional issues into what ought to be purely logical decisions. So, this has been a largely left-brained, analytical chapter. Chapter 13, the final chapter in our program, will be quite different. There we'll look at wealth, income, and financial freedom from a much different perspective.

THE FUTURE OF WEALTH

This is the final chapter in our journey. In Chapter 1, we spent some time discussing the definition of passive income and also its primary purpose. We determined that the destination of passive income is not really financial riches but financial freedom. The destination is not having the power to do everything rather it's freedom from having to do anything. Although we may think of wealth as driving expensive cars and vacationing in exotic locations, a great many wealthy individuals would agree with the more modest goals we've set in these chapters.

Not long ago a book called *The Millionaire Next Door* (Taylor Trade Publishing, 2010) reached the bestseller list. The authors—Thomas Stanley and William Danko—discovered that most millionaires really could be just like your neighbors. They don't jet around the world or eat caviar for breakfast. Most of them live in average neighborhoods in average houses. In other words, they live below their means. Their lifestyles are not frugal, but not extravagant, either—and they think saving money is as much fun as getting it. But they do take their investments very seriously through study on their own as well as advice from financial advisors. Yet the typical millionaire is not a person with a stellar academic record. The majority don't have MBAs or other advanced degrees. Some didn't go to college, and a few didn't even finish high school.

As the book further points out, most wealthy people are self-employed or own a business. They don't like to work for other people. Most are self-made success stories. The majority of millionaires received no family money and do not plan to give their own children a lot of money. They want their children to succeed the same way they did, on their own.

But here's the most striking fact about these wealthy people: They're happy about their lives. They feel good about where they are and where they're going. Looking at that from the outside, that might not seem very noteworthy. After all, if people are rich, why shouldn't they be happy? But the deeper question is, Are they happy because they're rich, or are they rich because they're happy?

The answer to that is very important for gaining a perspective on passive income—both in your own life and for those who come after you. In this final chapter, we'll be looking at the connection between happiness and passive income, and we'll see what you can do to optimize that connection.

GET RICH, STAY HAPPY?

In our society, the link between being rich and being happy is mostly taken for granted. Relatively little research has been devoted to it.

But a major 2003 study by the University of California at Berkeley showed that the financial component of money and happiness is a very individual matter. As the researchers put it, "We did find that income had a positive relationship with a sense of well-being and satisfaction among individuals high in extrinsic orientation." In plain English, that means if you value the things money can buy, then money will make you happy. But what about people with a less materialist outlook? If the most important things in your life are personal fulfillment, creativity, or spiritual seeking, will money fail to make you happy?

Well, not only will it fail to make you happy, but it might actually make you unhappy. For example, if people chose a career solely because they thought it would make them rich, they'd probably feel good if they did get rich. But if they chose a career because they wanted to make the world better for humanity, and then they got rich anyway, they could feel quite confused. In fact, they could feel downright depressed. Among those with a strong tendency to value work because they enjoyed it or it fulfilled them, those making more money were less happy than those making relatively little money.

Even in areas of life outside their primary career, receiving monetary rewards for doing an enjoyable task can make the task less enjoyable. Our sense of fulfillment and personal reward in life is actually very fragile, and money can easily destabilize it. People have a fundamental need to feel as though their actions are freely chosen. We all need to feel that we're not doing things just for the money—unless we actually are. Simply put, if we make the choice to sell out, that's one thing. But if we feel as if we've sold out without ever having made that choice, the feeling can be very different, and considerably worse.

MORE MONEY, MORE PROBLEMS

As you might expect, the negative side effects of wealth become more pronounced as you move up the financial ladder. A person who needs money to buy food will not feel the same about a financial windfall as a person who already has a million dollars in the bank. At higher income levels, psychological and emotional needs start to displace physical necessities. So the more successful you become financially, the more careful you need to be in other areas.

Again, this precept has implications not only for our own lives, but for those who we hope will benefit from our legacy. Inheriting a substantial amount of money from a rich uncle is usually a good thing in someone's life, but it's not always a good thing. The fact is, there are other values in our lives besides the financial ones. We need to be aware of how organizing our lives around making money can affect those values. Take Tyler's story as an example:

I always tried to have two different sets of goals—one set for my work and another for my life outside work. I had seen lots of entrepreneurs get confused around this. When people go into business for themselves, they mix their financial objectives with personal ones. So, I always felt that my business had only one goal, which was to make money. And the way to do that was by developing and retaining customers. After all, if you don't make money, you go out of business. You can't grow. You can't do anything. It's over.

My personal goals were a lot more diverse. I wanted early retirement, job satisfaction, career security, and financial independence, and to be my own boss. But now I see that what I thought were personal goals were actually all about my work. It's strange how that happened, because I had always been very concerned about dividing things into categories and keeping one category separate from another. That's why I always tried to work on my business but not in my business. My business was custom-made signs, but I did not make the signs. I hired people to make signs. I worked on my business by being on the outside, spending time with customers and potential customers. I was always aware of being with people who might have a reason to buy, if not immediately, then sometime in the future.

Because of the difference I saw between working on my business and in my business, I knew that my employees were an absolutely critical element of success. In a way, I saw them as if they were my *customers—because if you treat employees as your best customers, then they will treat your customers extremely well. If you treat your employees poorly, then they will treat your customers the same way. When my company exceeded $200,000 in monthly sales for the first time, the payoff was an all-expense-paid trip to Las Vegas for everyone in the firm.*

As an entrepreneur, I always felt it was extremely important to be a leader. Your employees have to be able to depend on you just as you have to depend on them to run your business. A lot of company owners know something about their product or service, but they lack other business skills. Some are not good leaders or managers, and others won't pay to get the right people.

When it came to investing, I can see now that my tendency to compartmentalize things got in the way. I wanted to develop some passive income for myself through stocks, and I wanted to invest in mutual funds for my family. I ran into a significant problem that cost me money. I thought that if I could turn this all over to an investment manager, just as I had turned the operational side of my business over to my employees. I thought that if I found someone who had a good reputation and I paid him top dollar, I could be hands-off about this and go on like before. But as it turned out, when I looked at the results, I was very disappointed. The investments had in no way outperformed the market as a whole. If I was just going to be on the Dow Jones Average, I could have done that myself and saved the big fees I paid my advisor.

If you have investments aimed toward passive income, you have to see them as a third category in addition to business and personal life. You can't see this as just another aspect of one thing or the other because it is something all its own. So you have to learn to spend time on it without spending too much time on it, especially at the beginning. Make those moves and learn how to navigate this third category. Even if you don't have any money coming in at first, at least you can be confident that you're on the right track.

chapter thirteen · the future of wealth

HAVE CERTAINTY IN YOUR SKILLS AND GOALS

One of the problems with being smart and successful in one area is believing you can do the same in all areas. Tyler obviously had evolved a system that worked well in his business, but it was not transferable to his investments. He is clearly a very hard worker and a dynamic thinker, but he misunderstood the meaning of passive investment. You are only passive in the sense that you passively accept the money. You're not passive in turning your investments over to somebody at the outset, and then more or less forgetting about them. Remember, the "millionaires next door" enjoyed studying and stayed on top of their investments. The trick is learning to do this without turning it into another full-time job. It can be done—but as Sheila discovered, sometimes it costs a little money to learn the business. Here is her story:

They say that necessity is the mother of invention, and it really is. From the moment I learned that I was pregnant, I knew that I wanted to stay at home and take care of my baby. I did not want to return to work full time. I absolutely wanted to stay home, but I also wanted to provide a supplemental income to our household. Actually, I had to provide some income. That's just the reality of the area we live in.

So every day I was online looking for stay-at-home jobs. However, I discovered that there are not a great number of legitimate work-at-home opportunities. There are a lot of phony ones but not many real ones. I even responded to work-at-home ads at the back of a baby magazine, but they also were scams. So finally I came up with an idea of my own.

From the very first I was sure my idea would work—and also from the very first my goal was to turn this into a passive income source. That way, I would be able to contribute to the family budget without having to spend most of my time working. I knew it wouldn't happen all at once, but I also knew it would not take very long. That's how confident I was in my idea.

When I was expecting my first child, I was interested in prenatal and infant stimulation—especially classical music effects in baby development. I was spending a lot of time on the internet researching pregnancy, prenatal care, and development. Once I was on an expecting moms' board, and they were talking about playing classical music for their babies. I had an idea that could combine two interests: the desire to stay home with my baby and my focus on infant development and stimulation.

Around that time, there was a lot of buzz about the first 12 months to three years of a baby's development. I began looking at different infant stimulation and prenatal products. I also was aware of those junky baby gift baskets that people buy when they can't think of anything else. There's nothing worthwhile in them—just little tubes of lotion and powder. But it costs about $60 to send one to family and friends. All the members in my family got one when they had a baby. People spent good money to send them, and they were things that nobody could use.

So I thought I could put together some things that actually benefit an infant, preferably with long-term benefits. My idea was to put together a classical music CD and some development toys. I made them affordable, starting at $20. A really good business started with those gift packages. There were five for babies and five for birthday gifts. The products increased as the business grew—and in much less time than I expected, I was able to license my brand to virtually every hospital gift shop in my state. And I'm sure it won't stop at the state border either. Meanwhile, my family has a really substantial source of passive income, and we're able to save a good part of it, too.

Unlike many entrepreneurs, Sheila succeeded despite limited experience in business—or maybe because her experience was limited. She is also unusual in that her commitment to her business was very contained. She didn't want to devote her life to this. She just wanted to generate some income so she could use her time the way she really wanted. She was also extremely confident from the very start that she

chapter thirteen • the future of wealth

would be able to meet her goals. This is an almost ideal mindset for creating a passive income.

BE OPEN TO OPPORTUNITIES IN YOUR OWN BACKYARD

Not everyone can have Sheila's combination of certainty and serenity, but in this case it paid off well. As someone once said, "Success is not always overcoming difficulties. Sometimes it's finding easiness." It doesn't have to be hard, and it can even be fun. You have to be open to what the universe lays out in front of you sometimes. And often, you'll find it right in your own backyard. Or in Janice's case, right in her own classroom. Check out her story:

For 30 years, I worked in mechanical engineering for a Fortune 100 company. When I retired, I had no intention of sitting around the house, and I don't fish or play golf, either. So I got a job teaching math at a local community college. Every day I did my best to generate understanding of mathematics in my students. But at the end of every class, I was overwhelmed by all the students who asked for extra help. Their goal was to transfer to the state university, and they were extremely focused on getting the best grades they possibly could.

I spent a lot of spare time working with my students one-on-one. There was such a strong demand that I would have to tutor full time in order to reach them all. Then I had the idea of creating a business to meet student demand for extra assistance. But I was an engineer and a teacher, not an entrepreneur. I knew my field, but I had always been an employee of a large organization. I didn't know the first thing about starting and managing a business.

I spent a year checking out the competition. I had always been interested in the way one company could succeed just by copying another company, with maybe just a single area of difference. How different is one cell phone from another? Does anybody choose an airline because they really prefer it to a different airline? The main buying decisions are based on price and convenience—so I decided to emphasize that. I was going to promote my tutoring service as a kind of neighborhood business. And since many of my clients would come from the community college, my first employees were also graduates of that system. They were people who had successfully transferred to the state university, just as my students wanted to do.

I rented a small storefront near the college and opened the doors with four students already signed up. Soon I was offering math, English, special education, and economics. I opened other learning centers, always within a few blocks of a community college. It was just like Wendy's opening across the street from McDonald's. After four years, I now employ 30 tutors and more around exam times. And I have never advertised. All my clients come from referrals.

At this point in my career, my goals are different from what they would have been earlier. In as few words as possible, I want to sell this business. I want to open a few more satellite branches and then get bought out by one of the national tutoring organizations. I have such a strong following that whoever buys me will pretty much own the market in this area. So I'm confident I'll be able to meet that goal.

With whatever I make from that sale, I want to create investments that will bring passive income to my kids, who are in the middle of raising their families. I hope that they will save some of that income or invest it, but that's really up to them. I know they're concerned about college costs down the road, so I hope some of the money will go to that. I also hope they look into the benefits of the community college system, which has certainly been of great benefit to me.

Janice is very different from most entrepreneurs. Instead of trying to find a business opportunity, the opportunity seemed to find her. With no need of income for herself, passive or otherwise, she will be able to help her family far into the future. This is a legacy in the true sense. It's about money, but it's also about happiness.

FIND YOUR HAPPY PLACE

According to Charlie Brown, happiness is a warm puppy. According to half the self-help books in America, happiness is a net worth like

Warren Buffet's. And according to the other half of the self-help books, happiness is inner peace and a weekly yoga class. So what is happiness? What is fulfillment? And what, if anything, do they have to do with money in general and with passive income in particular?

There's no doubt that in the United States and in other industrialized countries, happiness is often equated with wealth. Economists measure consumer confidence on the assumption that the resulting figure says something about progress and public welfare. The gross domestic product, or GDP, is routinely used as shorthand for the well-being of a nation.

But some places take a very different approach. In the small Himalayan kingdom of Bhutan, for example, the national priority is not the GDP but the GNH, or gross national happiness. The king of Bhutan has been instituting policies aimed at raising this measurement as high as possible. This means spreading the benefits that would normally go to the wealthy across the entire society. It also means questioning the meaning of wealth itself.

Around the world, economists, social scientists, corporate leaders, and bureaucrats are developing new ways to measure quality of life. These will take into account not just the flow of money, but also access to health care, free time with family, conservation of natural resources, and other noneconomic factors. The goal is to return to a richer definition of the word *happiness*. After all, that's the word that the signers of the Declaration of Independence had in mind when they included "the pursuit of happiness" as an inalienable right. They said it was equal to liberty and life itself. And it's worth noting that the inclusion of the word *happiness* in the Declaration did not occur without argument. An earlier draft referred to, "Life, liberty, and property"—as in an SUV and a second home in Colorado. But happiness eventually won out.

A similar concept focused on happiness and fulfillment in the early 1970s, when a book called *Small Is Beautiful: Economics As If People Mattered* by E. F. Schumacher became a huge bestseller. That ended abruptly with a gas crisis, followed by a burst of consumer-driven economic growth. That growth has continued to this day, often propped up by deficit spending by both private individuals and the federal government.

Yet many experts say this explosion of materialism will eventually lead us in another direction. In the early stages of a climb out of poverty, for a household or a country, incomes and contentment grow at the same pace. But beyond a certain point, about when annual income passes the equivalent of $30,000, happiness does not keep up. Even more striking, beyond a certain level of wealth, people appear to redefine happiness—which also means redefining wealth.

PARTING THOUGHTS

The purpose of this book has been to introduce you to the concept of passive income and to present some of the most reliable means for creating and sustaining it. But there seems to be an evolutionary mechanism that drives people to ever-higher goals. In the United States, we've passed the point in which our survival depends on aggressive and acquisitive behavior. This is a relatively new situation for human beings to be in—and the question becomes: How can we raise our quality of life, when increasing our income is no longer the most important factor?

To raise your income, to create new forms and resources of income, here are some things to remember. Invest in yourself through intellectual property. Take advantage of the moneymaking opportunities in internet technology. Buy income-producing real estate. Invest wisely in the stock market. Take out some life insurance policies. But don't stop at any single point on the map. The ultimate destination—true financial freedom—is still under construction. You yourself are building it with every forward step you take. Only you can say what it will finally look like or where it will be—because the destination is different in every person's heart.

RESOURCES

Some portions of this book originally appeared in *Start Your Own Business, Seventh Edition* (Entrepreneur Press, 2018), *Moonlighting on the Internet* (Entrepreneur Press, 2016), and on entrepreneur.com. To read the articles in their entirety, you can visit the links below:

Allen Moon. Entrepreneur contributor. "How to Start a Business Online." www.entrepreneur.com/article/175242

R.L. Adams, Entrepreneur contributor and founder of WanderlustWorker.com. "How Social Media Marketing

Generated $7 Million in Affiliate Sales for This Entrepreneur." www.entrepreneur.com/article/294084

Justas Markus, Entrepreneur guest writer and blogger. "13 Easy Investment Apps and Websites for Millennials." www.entrepreneur.com/slideshow/300579

Brian Hughes, Entrepreneur guest writer and CEO of Integrity Marketing and Consulting. "Two Strategies for Making Money Day Trading with a Bit Less Risk." www.entrepreneur.com/article/278184

R.L. Adams, Entrepreneur contributor and founder of WanderlustWorker.com. "15 Property Management Tips for Entrepreneurs Seeking Passive Income from Real Estate." www.entrepreneur.com/article/304577

Nicolette Amarillas, Entrepreneur Guest Writer and Founder of Expansive Voice. "How to Turn Your Side Hustle Into a Full-Time Gig." www.entrepreneur.com/article/315497

Sarah Max, Entrepreneur contributor. "Direct Selling Goes Social, Retools for Millennial Generation." www.entrepreneur.com/article/242306

Devlin Smith, Entrepreneur contributor. "Seven Tips for Network Marketing Success." www.entrepreneur.com/slideshow/299715

Kim Lachance Shandrow, Entrepreneur contributor. "10 Questions to Ask When Franchising Your Business." www.entrepreneur.com/article/247594

Mark Siebert, author of *Franchise Your Business* and *The Franchisee Handbook*. "The Nine Advantages of Franchising." www.entrepreneur.com/article/252591

ABOUT THE AUTHOR

Nightingale-Conant is the world leader in personal development, spiritual growth, wealth building, mind development, and wellness content. The company provides audiobooks, courses, seminars, and videos from notable authors like Brian Tracy, Jack Canfield, Deepak Chopra, Jim Rohn, and Zig Ziglar among many others. Access the full catalog at www.nightingale.com.

INDEX